**They couldn't kill him, because he was already one of**
# THE WALKING DEAD

## RIFLEMAN

As his fire team's automatic rifleman, Craig Roberts used an infrared scope to sight the enemy and shoot to kill. In the trenches and on patrol he became a deadly force with his M-14.

## RECON LEADER

With a ragtag band of Vietnamese ARVN rangers, he led a long-range recon into uncharted territory called the Valley of the Shadow of Death. Trapped by an entire VC company under punishing fire, Roberts kept his Rangers together, scored enemy kills—and brought the entire patrol out alive.

## SNIPER

Asleep in daylight, awake at night, Roberts emerged in darkness to stalk the enemy and kill. Armed with a Winchester rifle, hunting the VC on their own turf with their own methods, he beat them at their own lethal game—and helped prove American muscle in a new kind of war.

# THE WALKING DEAD

## CRAIG ROBERTS
### AND
## CHARLES W. SASSER

**POCKET BOOKS**

New York   London   Toronto   Sydney

An *Original* Publication of POCKET BOOKS

POCKET BOOKS, a division of Simon & Schuster, Inc.
1230 Avenue of the Americas, New York, NY 10020

ISBN 13: 978-0-671-65777-2
ISBN 10: 0-671-65777-1

First Pocket Books printing January 1989

11  10  9  8  7  6  5  4

POCKET and colophon are registered trademarks of
Simon & Schuster, Inc.

For information regarding special discounts for bulk purchases,
please contact Simon & Schuster Special Sales at 1-800-456-6798
or business@simonandschuster.com

Cover design by Jon Valk

Printed in the U.S.A.

This book is dedicated to all the men
who have gone to foreign wars and fought bravely—
and to those they left behind on the fields of battle.

"No, thank you, we don't want food, sir; but couldn't you take an' write a sort of 'to be continued' and 'see next page' o' the fight? We think that someone has blundered, an' couldn't you tell 'em how? You wrote we were heroes once, sir. Please, write we are starving now."

—"The Last of the Light Brigade"
Rudyard Kipling

# Foreword

The trucks lurched to a halt in front of regimental headquarters, red dust settling over the green canvas of the tents. I stood wearily, threw my pack onto the ground, and crawled down the side of the six-by.

The Gunny shouted orders and the company—or what was left of it—began to form up in an almost forgotten in-ranks formation.

Eight months in the field had taken its toll. No sleep, little food, and nonexistent basic medical care showed on our shrunken, battle-hardened frames. Like skeletons in green nylon rags, we faced the front.

Two Air Force Air Policemen stood across the road behind coils of concertina wire, staring at us. We could hear them when they finally spoke—

"Would you look at that?" said the first.

"Yeah, those guys look like *walkin' death*," said the other.

They weren't the first to use the term for the Ninth Marines, and they wouldn't be the last.

We landed young, eager, and full of ideals. We left old, so very old . . . tired and much wiser. We had marched a thousand miles, waded a hundred paddies, and saw things no man should see. We have killed, and in turn, been killed. Yet those of us who survive today know one thing above all . . . *We did our duty*.

> —L/Cpl William C. Roberts
> 3rd Btn., 9th Marines
> Vietnam, Spring, 1966

# Da Nang T.A.O.R    1965–66

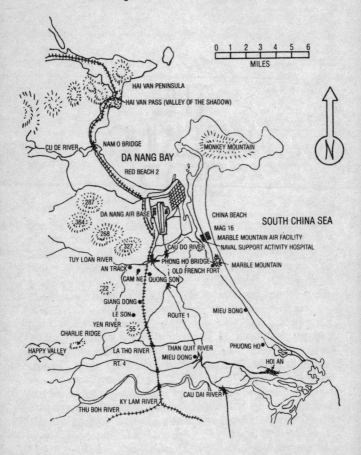

0 1 2 3 4 5 6
MILES

N

HAI VAN PENINSULA

HAI VAN PASS (VALLEY OF THE SHADOW)

CU DE RIVER
NAM O BRIDGE
MONKEY MOUNTAIN

DA NANG BAY

RED BEACH 2

287

DA NANG AIR BASE

CHINA BEACH

SOUTH CHINA SEA

MAG 16

364

MARBLE MOUNTAIN AIR FACILITY

268

NAVAL SUPPORT ACTIVITY HOSPITAL

327

CAU DO RIVER

TUY LOAN RIVER

PHONG HO BRIDGE

MARBLE MOUNTAIN

AN TRACK

OLD FRENCH FORT

CAM NE

QUONG SON

22

GIANG DONG

LE SON

MIEU BONG

YEN RIVER

ROUTE 1

CHARLIE RIDGE

55

HAPPY VALLEY

LA THO RIVER

THAN QUIT RIVER

PHUONG HO

RT. 4

MIEU DONG

HOI AN

KY LAM RIVER

CAU DAI RIVER

THU BOH RIVER

# Chapter 1

THE CROTCH, the by-God U.S. Marines, didn't tell you shit. The thinking behind keeping you in the dark—like a mushroom, kept in the dark and fed horse shit—was that if you were a grunt you didn't need to know the "Big Picture." All you had to do was follow orders, hit the beach, and keep going. In the Marines, there was no word for retreat or retrograde. Where the hell could you go? Back into the sea?

It was July 9, 1965. I was nineteen years old—PFC Craig Roberts, the Crotch, like my old man in WWII, the Big One he liked to call it. From the bow railing of the Navy WWII assault ship USS *Pickaway*, thirty miles out to sea, I could smell the cooking fires, dead fish, rot, and human shit of Vietnam. Beyond that expanse of shimmering blue water, turning green as it reached the land, were the enemy, the gooks, the Viet Cong, or VC as they were being called. My country and LBJ said they were commies trying to take over and needed their asses kicked.

The by-God Marines could do some ass-kicking.

The tropical sun and sea air on the way over from Okinawa

had started bleaching my short crop of blond hair to a dirty white. I was already boot camp tan and boot camp lean. I had to squint up through the sweat in my eyebrows at the Mike and Poppa boats bobbing in the sea alongside the ship waiting for their cargoes of Marines. The collar of the Navy lifejacket pressing against the back of my helmet kept my chin pushed down. The heavy pack rode in a darkness of sweat on my back. Someone once observed that a Marine was nothing but a life support system for his rifle; my M-14 was doing fine.

Christ, it was hot. The sun itself became a burden. We would get to know it like we would get to know the shit-smeared punji stakes, the Malaysian whips, the black-pajamaed gooks who sniped at us during the night and turned farmer again with the rising sun, but we would never get used to it. It sucked the moisture through the pores in my skin until I felt like a fish left on a gray and weathered pier.

Hot.

"Ladies, get your fuckin' asses in gear. We goin' to a war, Marines, not some old lady's tea party. You want to live, make goddamned sure you are locked and loaded when them boats hit the beach and the gates drop. Make goddamned sure."

The deck of the *Pickaway* was alive with gray green utility uniforms; it echoed with the clank of rifles and bayonets and E-tools and K-bars; it vibrated with the shouting of the sergeants. The Second Battalion, Ninth Marines, was going ashore in one of several WWII-style beach landings the Ninth Marine Expeditionary Brigade had made since LBJ committed the first land troops to Vietnam five months ago. We heard the VC had fourteen combat units within fifty miles of Da Nang. Most of them would probably be waiting for us on China Beach when we landed.

That was what "Hanoi Hannah" said. We sometimes picked her up on Radio Hanoi on our way over:

". . . Those of you men who are now approaching the People's Republic of Vietnam with the Ninth Marine Expeditionary Force, be sure to say good-bye to your loved ones in your letters. Many of you will die today or tomorrow. There is a squadron of MiG fighters coming to greet you and a submarine from the People's Republic of China watching you right this minute. . . ."

Sergeant Shireman said Hanoi Hannah was full of shit, like Tokyo Rose in WWII or Peking Polly in Korea. Still, it was a bit unnerving to be talked to by the enemy.

I watched Sergeant Shireman where he was helping our platoon commander, Lieutenant Rowe, get the landing nets ready for us to go over the sides. The sonofabitch was grinning. Now that was a pair—Sergeant Shireman and Lieutenant Rowe.

Rowe was short and stocky with a baby face, so quiet-spoken as to be almost diffident. He was new at the game, having come to the platoon just before it left Camp Pendleton to sail for Okinawa and then Vietnam. Sergeant Shireman had formed the platoon that day on the tarmac beneath the California sun. Lieutenant Rowe waited stiff and well creased nearby.

Sergeant Shireman said, "Men, this is Lieutenant John Rowe. This is your new platoon commander. He just graduated from Quantico. He played football."

He turned to the officer. "Sir, the platoon is formed. They're awaiting your command."

Lieutenant Rowe squared his corners and stood at attention centered on the platoon. Even though he raised his voice to address his very first command, his speech remained soft and unsure of itself around the edges.

"Sergeant Shireman tells me I have a good platoon of men," he began. "We're not just going to be good—we're going to be the best the Marine Corps has ever seen."

I kept my eyes locked straight ahead, but mentally they rolled back in my head. Oh, God, not another one of those.

"We will be the best. I will help you to become the best."

The grim look on Sergeant Shireman's face promised quick and certain retribution if one single eyeball clicked off center.

"I have an open-door policy, men," Lieutenant Rowe

15

said. "If any of you have a problem, you are welcome to come directly to me with it."

He gave his pep talk, then he marched off, squaring his corners. Sergeant Shireman waited until he was out of hearing range. Then he said, "All right, listen up, shitbirds. If I find one of you shitbags going to see that lieutenant without going through me first, I'll have your balls in my locker. There ain't no reason for you to bother that lieutenant. If I can't handle it, it can't be handled."

Sergeant Shireman was Hotel Company, Second Platoon's Right Guide—like an *assistant* platoon sergeant, but there was no doubt in the platoon who *really* ran it. Sergeant Shireman did. He did not look much like John Wayne—he was a lean six feet tall, about 30, with black, short-cropped hair and high cheek bones framing eyes so dark and piercing they gave him the look of a hawk eying its prey—but he was a John Wayne kind of guy. He walked into the platoon bay and you could almost hear the theme song from *The Sands of Iwo Jima.* You might call some of the other sergeants by their first names, but not him. He said Sergeant *was* his first name. He started more bar fights by himself than any normal platoon of Marines. It was part of his image.

"If I ever get married," he said, "the broad had better wear combat boots, have a gun collection, and stand to attention, by God, when the American flag goes by."

"And fuck?"

"And fuck for Old Glory and the Corps."

He said we were going to have a "hot" landing on China Beach. He didn't mean the sun either. He also promised we'd be home telling war stories by Christmas.

"NOW HEAR THIS . . . NOW HEAR THIS . . ."

Nothing happened aboard ship unless the PA system announced it first.

"PREPARE FOR DISEMBARKATION . . . FIRST PLATOON, INDIA COMPANY TO RED THREE . . . SECOND PLATOON, HOTEL COMPANY, TO BLUE TWO . . ."

Numbers inside colored blocks painted on the ship's deck designated stations. The ship rolled in the gentle swell while the landing boats around her bobbed, out of synch, like quick, active chicks. I caught hurried glimpses of the faces of the others in my squad—Frenchy Michaud, Roland O'Brien, Pete Yates, Dave Bruce, Smitty, and the others. Sweat poured out of their helmets and down their faces. Only Sergeant Shireman seemed to be having a good time. The rest of us kept glancing toward the thread of distant beach where the VC waited with machine guns ready.

"A piece of cake," said Frenchy, his Montreal-thick accent as cloying as the heat.

I took another look at their faces to see if they might be feeling the same things I was. I decided they were. We were a bit awed by the prospect of combat, but we were also young and somewhat thrilled at the promise of adventure and a chance to do our duty to country, as our fathers had in the Big One and our uncles in Korea. Growing up beneath the dark cloud of the Cold War, living under the threat of communist expansion, we were finally getting our chance to stop the commies by going to a foreign and exotic land and battling the evil on its doorstep. It was a Noble Cause.

I wondered how Rudyard Kipling would have viewed it. Whereas I saw Bibles being tucked into some of the other packboards, I shoved a worn copy of Kipling deep into mine. Kipling knew about fighting men. He had been to his war; now I was going to mine.

Sergeant Shireman came by.

"Saddle up, ladies. First four over the side. Second four, stand by."

Surprisingly enough, Lieutenant Rowe led the way. We clung to the nets like rats as the rocking of the ship banged us against the sides. We had to let go and drop the last distance into the landing craft. Spray sloshed up between the *Pickaway* and the boats, drenching the crowded men. As soon as a boat was full, it steamed away and slowly made a wide circle with the others, waiting to form the assault. I found myself asshole-to-belly button with the rest of my platoon, so packed in I was gasping for a breath of air.

17

"Goddamnit, get your heads down. Don't be peeking over the sides. You want your fuckin' heads shot off?"

I found that funny if a bit unnerving; the Poppa boats were made of plywood.

The big engines had been idling. Suddenly, they began to rev. My boat vibrated like a shockless old Ford over the washboard dirt roads in eastern Oklahoma where I grew up. I took a chance and copped a peek over the side. It was awesome. Long lines of gray flat-bowed boats had lined up across the sea. On some signal, their props kicked up a giant washing machine of water and we charged toward the beach, leaving wakes that broadened behind us and made even the *Pickaway* start to bob like a fishing cork. Spray hissed over the bow.

All that was missing was the bugles.

And the rest of the Navy. "I thought they were supposed to shell it or something to soften it up for us," some worrywart said.

"Marines don't need that sissy shit," Sergeant Shireman growled. "Lock and load. Lock and load."

Some Spanish guy in front of me crossed himself. A machine gunner fumbled nervously with an ammo belt in an assault pack. He finally got the feed tray closed and braced himself for the rush up the beach under fire.

"One hundred meters to sand!"

For the first time, I felt something stirring in my guts, like some undefined furry creature just waking from a long hibernation—or just being born. Two Navy machine gunners in the bow crouched behind their light Browning.

Still no fire from the beach. The gooks must be waiting for the landing gates to drop in the surf.

The boats hit with a jolt that jammed us against each other. Then the gates dropped. I glimpsed a sandy strip backed by palm trees, almost like a postcard from Hawaii or Miami Beach—"Wish You Were Here."

"Beach! Go, goddamnit, go! Go! Go go go go go go go!"

The waters of Asia were warm. They sucked at my waist as, caught up in the excitement, I charged with the other

Marines toward dry sand, screaming and yelling rebel war cries. Ready for action. Expecting it. *Wanting* it.

I thought I would never escape the sea. As soon as I felt solid land beneath my boots, I dove into it face first and did a combat roll to the left to keep the VC from marking my position. I quickly unfolded the bipod on my automatic rifle and swung the gun ready for action, swiveling it back and forth across the front of brown white sand and palm trees and shimmering heat devils, my eyes darting and busy.

Where were the human hordes?

Phil Leslie kicked up sand as he ploughed onto his belly next to me. He was my ammo bearer.

All I heard was my heart pounding in my trigger finger and the cries of Marines as they hit the beach belly down and heads and rifles up.

Then I saw the kid. He was about eight years old with an eight-year-old's grin, yellow skin, no shirt, and a baggy pair of too-short black trousers. My first gook. Holding out two bottles, he positioned himself directly in front of my weapon.

"Hey, Joe . . . you buy Co'Cola?"

"Wha' the fuck. . . ?"

I noticed the others. Kids and toothless old women who grinned like the kids. They were all up and down the beach— the enemy. Selling Cokes and beer and cigarettes. Sergeant Shireman was standing up scratching his crew cut and starting to grin. Frenchy and O'Brien slowly clambered to their feet and looked stunned. I stood up and stared at the kid.

"Buy Co'Cola, Joe? Buy Co'Cola?"

# Chapter 2

THE THING IS, if you are a grunt Marine and can't find any action, then you run until you do. When in doubt, take a hill.

"Let's go . . . go . . . *go!*"

Go? Where the fuck go?

Down the beach we went, trotting in full packs and combat gear past shirtless Seabees driving forklifts and stacking ammo cases on pallets and drinking Cokes, the kids and toothless old women smiling and bobbing their heads and running along with us, hawking their wares.

"Jee-suz Kee-rist!" That was O'Brien. He was always saying it. "This is fucking ridiculous."

I yelled at one of the Seabees as we clanged and rattled past, weapons at port arms: "Hey, squid. Where's the war?"

"How should I know? We just got here yesterday."

There had to be a hill around somewhere. Marines had to have their beaches and their hills. We came to Monkey Mountain and started climbing. What started out as a charge quickly panted down to a slow drudging walk. We slung arms and used our hands to pull ourselves up. Heat rode us like a jockey flogging a dying horse. Soaked with sweat, some of the men started falling out from heat.

"Pussies," Sergeant Shireman said, coming by.

The man wasn't human. He got by on less sleep than any of us, but he was always ready to go. Still grinning. The heat was nothing to grin at. It was like you put on all the clothes you owned, including combat boots, flak jacket, helmet, and pack, and then crawled into a sauna where you started digging holes in the ground and filling sandbags and wading through warm rice paddies and rushing up hills.

Monkey Mountain loomed in the center of an odd-shaped peninsula with the South China Sea on one side running around into Da Nang Bay on the other. The Da Nang airbase, still under construction, lay three or four miles to the southwest. By the time we struggled to the top of the mountain we couldn't give a fuck about looking at any airfield, even though providing security for it was purportedly the reason the Marines had landed. The VC could have kicked *our* asses. All we wanted to do was fall out and catch our breath. Marines were strung out down the mountain for a mile, all huffing and puffing and clanging and grunting and cursing their recruiters.

I had no reason to curse my recruiter; he hadn't lied to me. He'd resembled a uniformed gorilla with an armful of stripes, a chestful of ribbons, and hair so short he looked unshaven on top. He growled when I walked into the recruiting station fresh out of high school and tanned from the summer, a kid off the block. I almost turned back around and ran out, except Kipling had written about tough guys like him, all iron on the surface and heart in the middle. A warrior who could kill an enemy without batting an eye and die for a friend the same way.

"Well, uh . . ." I stammered.

"We don't offer nothin'," the gorilla snarled. Kipling may have been wrong about the heart in the middle. He kept staring at me like he could see right down into my guts, checking them out to see if I had any.

"We don't offer nothin'," he growled again, pushing back from his desk, "but I'll tell you *this,* lad. When you're in combat and you're standin' in the mud with fixed bayonets and no ammo and there's a thousand screaming Chinese commies charging up the hill toward you—*your buddy won't bug out on you.*"

That was how I ended up in the Marines climbing Monkey Mountain looking for a hill to take or a hill to defend. I was afraid to turn around and leave and let the Marine recruiter think I *didn't* have any guts.

Somebody was on top of Monkey Mountain ahead of us. The leading elements broke into a small clearing at the summit. We stopped and stared. A Marine lying on a cot in the open with his shirt off and wearing reflecting sunglasses slowly got up on one elbow and stared back in puzzled surprise. Behind him, another Marine huddled at a portable radar station; he yawned out a lazy grin.

What kind of war was this? We expected a "hot" landing and instead got Seabees driving forklifts like stevedores, kids hawking Cokes at the Dodger Stadium, and crew-cut Americans lounging on cots in the sun.

Looking as confused as the rest of us, Lieutenant Rowe went aside to get instructions through the radio. The radar team jumped up when Sergeant Shireman approached.

"Any action around here?" he demanded.

The grunt with the sunglasses pointed down the other side of the hill. "Jones here said he heard some shooting down that way last night."

Down that way was the way we went. The gray green caterpillar of Marines straggling up one side of the hill compressed and went tumbling and rolling down the other side. At the bottom of the hill, the sergeants got their platoons on line and we went pushing through grass taller than our heads. The blades of the grass were wide at the center and tapered off to sharp points. I made the mistake of grabbing it to push it aside and learned why elephant grass was sometimes known as knife grass.

Sergeant Shireman's hand shot up. We halted, crouching, listening. Voices drifted back to us on the oven's fan. The first fire-team leader signaled "Enemy ahead" by drawing the edge of his hand across his throat, then pointing in the direction of a line of brush ahead of us.

We crept forward until, on line, we broke out of the brush onto a dirt road. The road was lined with U.S. Marine Corps six-by trucks. One of the drivers flicked a cigarette away and walked toward us.

"It's about goddamned time. Where the hell you grunts been?"

Even Sergeant Shireman looked sheepish.

"Crawl your asses into these trucks and we'll take you to the war." The driver smirked.

War wasn't only confusion; it was boredom and drudgery, too. And hard work. Physical labor and waiting. Instead of hauling us off to adventure, the six-bys trucked Second Platoon down to the Da Nang harbor where American assault cargo ships rode heavy in a greasy scum. It was one hundred degrees with humidity to match when, disconcerted and leaden with disappointment, we began offloading the ships' cargo holds to start the big ammo dump at the Da Nang airfield. It was port-and-starboard duty, six hours on and six off, twenty-four hours a day, in and out of the holds like rats. The ships rode lighter on the water until the scum line on the hulls was six feet above the surface.

"Jee-suz Kee-rist, Roberts," exclaimed O'Brien, pointing into the water. "Look at the shit in the water. Ain't it *real* turds?"

Even with his unlikely Irish name, O'Brien was an Arab, swarthy and solidly built with black horn-rimmed glasses. When his grandfather emigrated to the United States, the family name had been Ali Baru, but the old man did not know how to write it in English. He found a piece of paper with the name George O'Brien written on it, and that was how the Arab O'Briens came to be.

Sergeant Shireman stood on deck in the sun smoking a cigarette and gazing absently across the bay. He had been working below with the rest of us and had stripped off his shirt. Muscles stood in gnarled knots across his shoulders and chest. He grinned slowly at the Arab.

"It's a perfect symbiotic arrangement," he said. Sergeant Shireman was always smarter than he let on.

"A what?" O'Brien asked.

"It works this way: You see, the gooks build their toilets so everything drops in the water. The shit in the water attracts fish who eat it. The gooks catch and eat the fish and then shit the fish back in the water for the fish to eat. It's perfect."

O'Brien made a face. "I ain't getting near no fish as long as I'm in this shit-for-brains country."

Even off duty, it was too hot to sleep. Nights, sweating and restless, we roamed the decks where it was cooler and watched the lights of the city. Huge floodlights mounted on the ships shone into the water to discourage enemy "frog men." The lights attracted hordes of sea snakes that writhed and tumbled in a murky hell below us.

Gradually, the ammo dump built up at the base of Hill 327, the highest piece of real estate west of the airfield. A Hawk guided missile company and a radar outfit dug in on top of the hill. After my platoon finished offloading the ships, we trucked away from the bay with the last crates of bullets to pull security for 327 until we could be drawn back into the battalion. Disappointed, I was beginning to think we were never going to see the war, that we'd end up offloading ships and drawing security and climbing already occupied hills for the duration. A week in-country and I hadn't even *heard* a shot fired. At this rate, the war would be over long before Christmas—if, in fact, it had ever begun.

After digging in at the bottom of the hill, we had nothing else to do except sit around, bored, helmeting water over our sweaty bodies from a little stream and shooting giant dragonflies with rubber bands.

The issuing of a new "ballistics" helmet provided a short diversion. It was supposed to deflect shrapnel and low-velocity bullets. O'Brien picked up one and looked it over.

"Frenchy, give me your K-bar," he said, after stomping the helmet and slamming it against the ground and generally giving it a testing.

He took aim with the knife and threw it. The knife pierced the helmet as though it were cardboard.

"Jee-suz Kee-rist," O'Brien said, picking up the helmet with the knife through it and showing it around. "Jee-suz Kee-rist."

Word came down at the end of the week. Tomorrow, Second Platoon would link up with company and leave the Da Nang enclave to cross the old "Rivière du Tourane," now the Da Nang River, to sweep and occupy a village complex called Duong Son. The VC were supposed to be at Doung Son. Sharpening stones and K-bars came out, and cleaning kits for the M-14s. It was the night before the young Marines of Second Platoon took the big step into combat; excitement and nervousness rippled like something fluid but solid through the ranks. There was a lot of talking in rushes—and a lot of silence in blocks.

# Chapter 3

UNTRIED AND UNBLOODED, anxious to taste combat but at the same time also just plain anxious, we looked like textbook combat Marines as the six-bys offloaded Hotel Company in bright morning sunshine on the airfield side of the Phong Le Bridge spanning the Da Nang River. Vietnam had not yet faded and frayed our utilities and everyone wore his Korean War–vintage flak jacket zipped up. The green nylon sleeveless vests filled with porcelain plates were stiff and hot and came just short of rattling like a dismounted knight's armor, but no one complained. Not yet.

I stood in the dust of the road while the company formed, and gazed with mixed curiosity and trepidation across the bridge that would come to symbolize the war for me. It was like I was about to experience a rite of passage. I did not understand it then, but after today, after crossing the bridge, I would never again view life the same way as before.

"I do not see any fook-ing Viet Cong," Frenchy Michaud said, squinting. There was a gentleness to the handsome French face, almost an innocence, that he pointed toward the land of the VC across the bridge. From Montreal, he had joined the Marines to obtain U.S. citizenship. He spoke fluent French and kept the charm of the accent when he switched to English.

It looked the same on the other side as on this side—rice paddies shining in the sun like green emeralds, bamboo thickets marking village perimeters, jungle clumped here and there like malignant growths on a jewel.

Sergeant Shireman studied Frenchy for a moment. "You won't see the VC until he wants you to," he said. "But you can bet he sees you."

We all took a second, longer look across the river.

"Second Platoon, listen up," Lieutenant Rowe shouted, as green as the rest of us but trying not to let on. "Once we cross the river, men, we are officially in enemy territory. So far, this is the limit of the advance from the Da Nang enclave. Be careful over there and keep on your toes." His voice rose: "The U.S. Marine Corps is going to war."

He paused as though for cheering offstage before proceeding with a briefing on our part of the mission. Hotel Company was going to sweep the village of Duong Son to drive the VC ahead of us to Golf Company advancing from the other side. We were the hammer, Golf the anvil.

We were finally going to kick some ass.

Nothing spectacular happened when we crossed the bridge in staggered formation except it *felt* different on the other side, in enemy country. We crossed two smaller bridges, a steel one and an old wooden one built across tributaries feeding the river, and then we angled off on a road built on an old railroad track bed. The road was elevated about ten feet above flooded rice fields stretching away on either side. Soon I spotted the bamboo tree line of a village on our left flank. With my platoon, the Second, running point, we trailed across dikes before finally getting on line at the edge of the village for the sweep. Nerves were stretched so tight you could almost hear them twanging, like out-of-tune banjo strings.

O'Brien was on my right, Pete Yates on the left. War, I

27

was to discover, boiled down to three or four things—who was on your left and right and who was directly in front shooting at you. I swallowed dry and made a point of rechecking my M-14. O'Brien's eyes looked like dark saucers behind his glasses. One of the saucers winked as we started the sweep into the village.

The hamlet was full of pigs, chickens, and water buffalo. The pigs resembled skinny Arkansas razorbacks, the chickens were even skinnier, while the only sound a beast as big as the water buf could make was a low, sad moan. Kids peeped wide-eyed out the doors of the grass huts. There were droves of kids under the age of about nine, and lots of women and ancients, but there were almost no males between the ages of twelve and thirty. I found that peculiar until it was explained how the males in that age group were either fighting with the VC or being conscripted by the ARVN—the Army of the Republic of Vietnam.

Stands of thorny bamboo, grown so close together that a chicken had trouble squeezing through, like privacy fences, sectioned off the dwellings. Marines entered huts apologetically and probed around in rice urns and jars and underneath mats, searching for evidence of Viet Cong—a concealed weapon, propaganda, a hidden entrance to a tunnel—while the occupants stood with inscrutable Asian faces and watched without comment, or, when questioned, rattled animatedly with ARVN interpretors.

I broke through a growth of bamboo onto a wide dirt path that meandered through the heart of Duong Son. Counterguerrilla Warfare School in Okinawa had taught us to beware of foot traps. Eying the path suspiciously as I advanced, I soon noticed several slight depressions that normal foot traffic appeared to have avoided. Taking out my K-bar, I knelt and dug around the edges testing for trip wires or pressure detonators, just like we'd been taught. While O'Brien and Yates watched, I located the edge of the lid and opened the trap to reveal a shallow hole teethed with sharp steel barbs. The barbs were smeared with human feces to cause infection. By the time we had uncovered three or four more punji pits we were starting to look upon the villagers in a different light.

"Those assholes would let us all step in 'em and not say a word," Pete Yates declared, offended. He was blond, wore glasses that matched O'Brien's, and spoke with an Ozark drawl that made you think he might be a little slow. He wasn't. He caught on quick.

"The *whole* village is Viet Cong," he said. "Every fucking man, woman, child, pig, chicken, and water buffalo—*Viet Cong.*"

We weren't so apologetic about intruding into the huts after that.

Sweeping, we linked up with Golf Company and found no VC caught between the hammer and anvil, just thin air. If Duong Son was overrun with Viet Cong, they had slipped out of our trap, as they were to do many times in the weeks ahead.

We swept back through, without seeing anything different, and started digging in on the village perimeter facing outward, as if we expected the VC to attack the village. That wasn't going to happen. Frenchy leaned on the short handle of his E-tool and wiped sweat. He was standing knee deep in his freshly evacuated fighting hole. He had a way of getting to the heart of any matter with just a few words.

"There ees more VC behind us in the village, *mon ami,* than in front of us," he said.

That observation added tension to the first of many long dark nights we were to endure waiting in holes dug in the ground.

My fire-team leader was a lithe and quiet black man from Stuttgart, Arkansas. Lance Corporal Dave Bruce was a spit-and-polish Marine who, back in the States, used to stay in on a Saturday night just to shine his boots and get his uniform and gear ready for the next week. You could count on him, though; a certain formal friendship had grown up between us. Since I was the fire team's automatic rifleman and needed to be near the leader, Bruce and I filled sandbags together and piled them in front of our hole in a bamboo treeline next to the main trail entering Duong Son.

The sun dropped just as we were finishing. Bamboo shadows stretched into a single purple mass that soon hid Yates and Smitty from our sight in the next foxhole. We were alone with the stars bright and the shadows dark and only an occasional sound from the village behind us.

It was easy, that first night, to keep awake. Bruce said, "Remember what they said about Korea?"

"What's that?"

"The gooks always attack about three A.M. when you are the most sleepy."

My eyes popped wide open.

Golf Company was dug in on perimeter to our right flank. It was about one-thirty when a series of four shots cracked from Golf's position. Instantly, everyone sprang up in his hole, eyes probing the darkness in front, weapons ready. Nothing happened.

Bruce said, "It ain't three A.M."

"I ain't never gonna sleep out here," I vowed.

The fire-team leader smothered a sleepy cough in his hand. "You'll sleep," he promised, but I saw his eyes wide and white in the starlight.

We settled back down—waiting. I had been hearing noises all night, but I marked them off as tricks played on me by an overactive imagination. Every time I stiffened, Bruce next to me grunted and looked around. I nudged him.

"Did you hear it?" I whispered.

"Man, I ain't hear nothing."

"There's something right out there. I *know* I heard it this time."

He listened. Nothing.

"Man," he grumbled, "we're fifty percent alert. It is my fifty percent time to sleep."

But, of course, he didn't sleep. I couldn't see his face, it was so dark, but I kept seeing his eyes popping white and wide. And I kept hearing, every few minutes, the rustling in the bamboo like some gook was trying to sneak up to the hole and slit our throats.

"Fuck it," Bruce said. "You're hearing things."

The rustling drew nearer. Bruce's eyes were closed. At least I couldn't see them reflecting the light from the stars. Bruce did not stir as I slowly and carefully drew my knees underneath and reached to grip my K-bar. There was *somebody* out there. I waited, my heart pounding against my ribs and in my throat. No gook was going to cut my throat without a fight.

I saw—*eyes*.

Every muscle in my body tautened instantly. With a desperate sound that was as much shriek as battle cry, I lunged at the enemy to grab him and sink my knife deep into his heart. Bruce shot out the other side of the hole on legs turned suddenly to coiled springs.

My knife blade was already stabbing into sand bags by the time my free hand grasped a handful of small furry body. I dropped it in alarm and fell back into the hole, panting and horrified.

"What the hell is that?" Bruce demanded.

I caught my breath. "The smallest, hairiest Viet Cong in Vietnam," I said, while the bamboo rat, squeaking with a fright of its own, scurried for cover.

That was the way the war started, and that was the way it went—we waited through the hot, muggy days; at night we hid in our holes like rats, protecting a Vietnamese village we were not sure *wanted* to be protected. After a while, we started getting used to the VC who probed the perimeter somewhere every night, firing a few rounds here and there to get return fire to mark our positions, as though they didn't already have maps drawn by the villagers. When it was my turn for fifty percent sleep, I curled up in the bottom of the hole and caught a few winks, secure in the knowledge that the snipers weren't really hitting anyone and that Bruce would wake me if anything ever did happen.

By this time I didn't expect anything to happen. What

could a few raggedy-ass gooks with cast-off weapons do to two full companies of well-trained and well-armed by-God U.S. Marines?

One night on watch I heard rustling in the bamboo again. O'Brien and Frenchy had been ragging me mercilessly about how I had, at risk of life and limb, fought off the vicious bamboo rat with just a knife and saved the platoon. I wasn't going to be fooled twice. I waited, unable to see a thing in the shadows out front, no matter how I strained to get my peripheral vision into play.

When the shots went off, I was looking directly into the fire blossoms. They weren't thirty meters away. I was hugging the ground by the time the echoes clapped against the village huts. It was the first time anyone had fired directly at me. I didn't know whether to be afraid or furious.

I heard Bruce yell, "Fire!"

That made up my mind for me. I opened up on full automatic, spraying the brush in front. An M-14 on automatic has a way of waltzing in your hands. All the other guys had given their rifles names. I called mine Matilda. Waltzing Matilda. I let Matilda waltz all through the bamboo.

Yates and Smitty opened up, too. We had a good little one-way firefight going by the time parachute flares popped and came floating down like miniature suns, sending harsh shadows scurrying and making the world black and white.

But there were no VC out there in front of us. There was nothing. Where the hell were they?

I huddled in my hole and brooded about it. That gook had almost got me, and now, almost every night, VC came sneaking along the bamboo line in the dark to take shots at us, for no reason I could discern other than to keep us awake and on edge. *My* VC, which was what I took to calling him, snapped shots at us from the same banana tree three or four nights during a week. We might not be able to see him, but coming back to that same banana tree was not the smartest thing in the world to do.

I had an idea for a little payback. I rounded up a one-pound block of TNT, some WD-1 commo wire, and some rusty barbed fencing. "A surprise for my VC," I explained to Bruce. "A message from mama."

I wrapped the block of TNT tightly with the rusty barbed wire and suspended it about six feet up the trunk of the tree so that when it exploded it would send wire shrapnel hurtling through the air like bullets. Taking the fuse from a grenade, I screwed it into the fuse well of the TNT. Then I ran commo wire from the grenade fuse pin back to my hole. All I had to do was give the wire a tug—no more banana tree.

Bruce and I grinned at each other when the sun started to go down. Now we had a purpose for waiting.

We waited two nights for the VC, who wasn't the smartest in the war, to show up again. Shortly after midnight on the third night two quick shots rang out from the banana tree. Bruce and I ducked into the hole and I yanked the wire. The explosion sent chunks of barbed wire buzzing over our heads and sprinkled pieces of bamboo and leaves into the hole on top of us. My ears rang from the concussion, but I was ecstatic.

"We got that sonofabitch!" I yelled.

It took several seconds for the squad leaders to regain fire control and cease the shooting. Then I listened. I found it incredible, but I heard the sounds of someone crawling in the bushes. *My* VC was getting away.

I lobbed a grenade at him. As soon as it detonated, I raised to listen some more. Bruce nudged me.

We heard moaning.

Strict orders had come down not to leave our positions after dark. There was no sleeping for either Bruce or me that night as we waited for daylight so we could go out to collect weapons and get our first real look at the enemy. We did not know it then, but the Viet Cong would go to great lengths to drag off their casualties. They even had men assigned during battle to drag off bodies with meat hooks. It proved demoralizing to us not to be able to see the enemy dead and wounded any more than we saw the enemy when he was alive.

The first thing I noticed at dawn was that the banana tree

had vanished. There was nothing left except a ragged stump. Impatiently, I waited for the sun to end the night's restriction to our holes. Shadows came, the sun kicked up red out of the rice paddy, and I went out eagerly to get *my* VC.

He was gone. There was nothing there.

It was going to be tough to kick ass when you were fighting ghosts.

# Chapter 4

THE BY-GOD MARINES might have kicked ass in big WW One-One, but it began to seem getting to kick ass in this place was going to take a hell of a lot longer. It was one *slow* war.

"Christmas, my ass," O'Brien the Arab grumbled. "Christmas what year?"

Sergeant Shireman just grinned at O'Brien and winked.

Like I say, in the Crotch they don't tell you shit. Mushrooms. We were dug in and waiting, but we never knew what we were waiting for. Maybe someone knew, someone back in a planning room with maps on the wall with colored pins stuck in them, but we didn't. What it might have been, we heard later, was that LBJ was back home in the States trying to justify sending in more troops to turn Vietnam into one big fort against the Indians. In the meantime, those of us who were already here were sitting around guarding wagon trains and settlers. Waiting for the cavalry to come.

The monsoon rains started. They started slowly and built up. The sun baked you all day and then, just before dark, a bunch of black clouds crawled over the sky and dumped basketfuls. The storms lasted for about an hour before the skies cleared off again against the stars, and everything steamed for the rest of the night. If you were not lucky enough or foresightful enough to get up a poncho hootch in time, then you were stiff and wet until the sun returned to turn the flame up from simmer to boil.

I was keeping an eye on a budding storm, but the downpour caught me before I could get back to the hootch I shared with Bruce. I ducked for the nearest shelter, underneath which Phil Leslie huddled alone. He moved over with a little grin to give me room to sit with him and then almost immediately returned his attention to the panorama laid out before us, the center of which was occupied by a young Vietnamese boy sitting on the back of a water buffalo in the rice paddies. Lightning stabbed, cracking, all around him, but the boy remained imperturbable. The furious rain beat up a mist that swirled and eddied around the boy and his dark mount, giving the scene the blurred-out mysterious look of a classic Asian painting.

While we watched, mesmerized, a tremendous crack of thunder accompanied by a bolt of lightning fired out of the low-hanging clouds seemed to supercharge the air around us. The lightning bolt struck the kid on the buffalo and knocked him about twenty feet through space. It left the buffalo standing, its head still lowered dumbly against the storm.

Villagers ran out to claim the kid's body. One of his Ho Chi Minh sandals remained in the young rice shoots after they carried him off. The Marines stood around, stunned by how suddenly the tragedy had occurred. The odor of brimstone hung in the rain. Leslie scratched his head, looked away briefly, then glanced back at the sandal.

"He was probably a VC anyhow," he murmured.

U.S. forces started expanding the perimeter around Da Nang to give us more operating room and to deny it to the VC. Golf Company stretched into our positions at Duong

Son, leaving Hotel Company free to move somewhere else. On line by platoons, Hotel swept across the rice in the first streaks of dawn until we reached a road. It was a long, stretched-out road march from there past three red brick towers sticking up like cigars. This was the brick factory, what we started calling the "Brick Piles." The towers could be seen from a great distance and made a fine landmark. Peasants wearing straw cone hats, their trouser legs rolled up past the knees from stomping straw and mud, stood up and, silent and inscrutable—some were undoubtedly VC— watched the foreign young warriors pass.

The sun inched higher and the sky turned hard and brassy. We slogged past grass huts and temples and graveyards with the graves like giant shallow bowls sunken into the earth. Sometimes, there was a sepulcher sitting outside a temple; later, after we were weary and contemptuous of all things Asian, Yates and O'Brien removed an elder's corpse from a sepulcher and filled it with water for a bath.

We left the road again and formed a lone line to chase any VC in the area ahead of us. Beyond a wide field divided by high dikes lay a small village shaded by palms and bamboo. Second Platoon angled off on a dike to reach our point for a sweep through the hamlet. Just as the platoon was about to line out again to link up with our adjacent sister platoons, four shots shattered the midday stillness.

I dived off the dike on the opposite side from the village and cautiously peeked above the edge to see what was happening. Everyone was hugging the side of the dike except for Sergeant Shireman, who, at the head of the platoon, was calmly down on one knee peering toward the village while he shaded his eyes with his hands. Like he might be looking for a street sign or waiting for a pedestrian light. That cool.

The ville was about five hundred meters away, a distance at which the sniper apparently felt safe. While we watched, a lone figure in black carrying a rifle erupted from hiding and made a dash from the village, following the top of a dike.

"He's mine."

Sergeant Shireman spoke as though he were out in Kansas

37

shooting pheasants, or like he had just jumped up an Oklahoma cottontail. For all his voice betrayed, that was not another human being out there. It was just a target.

"He's mine."

Like that. He leisurely brought his M-14 to his shoulder and sighted in on the running figure while everyone else watched. There was no way he could hit a moving target at that range.

The rifle cracked. To our amazement, the gook tumbled head over heels and then did not get up again. A lazy little puff of smoke drifted up in the sunshine over the sergeant's head. Sergeant Shireman smirked back at the platoon as though chiding us for doubting him.

No one was going to get this gook away from us, drag it off before we claimed it as a trophy. With a thundering spontaneous cheer, the entire platoon launched a crazy wild charge that went splashing across the flooded rice paddies toward the downed enemy, trying to beat the villagers who came charging out of their huts in the same maniacal way, like they had when lightning knocked the kid off the water buffalo.

Some of the locals beat us to the body, but we were so near they did not dare steal it. They crowded around and wailed and wrung their hands. We forced them back and crowded around the dead gook ourselves. We stood and looked down at the body—our first look at one of the little black-pajamaed men who ruled the nights. It seemed they were as vulnerable as any of us in the sunshine.

You always picture the enemy as being big and hairy and mean looking. This was a little guy in his late teens or early twenties. An outstretched hand would have spanned his chest. He had a godawful big red hole gouged through his rib cage, and his eyes, half-opened, were already glazed, as though the lights had been turned off because no one lived there anymore. His legs were stretched out like he was still running, but the sun bearing down on him had already started its shrinking process.

It struck me hard for the first time, seeing violent death,

that this was what war was all about—killing and being killed. It was a sobering thought to know that what we had done here in this rice paddy was the same thing these little men were trying to do to us.

The villagers continued to caterwaul and screech.

"They say he no VC," explained our ARVN interpretor. "They say he Popular Force, he PF. They say VC run away and he chase them."

An M-1 carbine lay next to the body. Sergeant Shireman picked it up. It had been fired. Four cartridges were missing from the clip. That told the story.

The ARVN grinned broadly. "I think he be numbah ten VC," he said. He pointed at the sergeant. "You numbah one shot. Boom!" he said, reenacting it. "Boom!" he said and laughed roundly.

"Yeah. Boom," said Sergeant Shireman, and led us away. No one looked back as the mourning villagers carried off our first VC to bury him.

Seeing your first dead gook, sobering as it was, was not nearly so grave an occasion as when Marines started getting it. Sergeant Shireman's gook must have been some kind of fanatic, or a mental case, to open fire on a company of Marines in full daylight and then jump up and run. Still, he had been shooting and running, and he got it fair and square. Not like our first Marine casualties, who weren't a clean kill like that for the VC. That, we came to understand quickly, was not how the VC played the game.

Death came to the Marines at night, in the dead of night, as they say, and it came for them unexpectedly, a dirty gross thing of terror.

H & S Company, Headquarters and Service, supporting the battalion, sent two wiremen out just before dark to string a commo land line between Golf Company dug in at Duong Son and a satellite platoon entrenched around an old school house. They only had to go about seven hundred meters across rice paddies where there was only a patch here and there of bamboo and jungle. They could be covered the entire distance by machine guns.

The wiremen disappeared nonetheless. Patrols sent out in the dark to find them returned at dawn bearing two sagging ponchos around which buzzed hordes of green flies. The young pallbearers were grim and silent, as were those Marines who gathered to watch the odd procession. The soft clump of weary footfalls, the clank of armed men, and the quick catch in breathing rhythm were the only sounds. Eyeballs clicked after the ponchos, following them. A thin trickle of blood spilled out the fold of one of the ponchos and made a plaintive thin inscription in red down the trail. The rest of the rescue patrol stepped in the blood.

Tales of what the rescue found joined in circulation other tales of VC atrocities, such as pregnant women left alive with their bellies ripped open, and children with their brains bashed out against trees as a lesson to villagers not to cooperate with the Americans. The patrol, to its horror, had found the wiremen strung up naked by their feet in a tree, like a brace of butchered hogs. Hundreds of knife wounds, evidence of torture, punctured the bodies. The Marines' testicles had been sawed off and jammed in their mouths as a warning to the rest of us.

Finding the mutilated wiremen changed our thinking. Suddenly, we saw the war clearly. This was no Geneva Convention war like we'd been told at Orientation. We weren't fighting enemy soldiers. We were exterminating animals.

# Chapter 5

IF YOU WERE A GRUNT, Vietnam was a narrowly focused war in which you never saw the "Big Picture." You moved first here and dug in, then you moved there, slogging through rice paddies, and dug in again among more rice paddies and bamboo and Arkansas pigs and skinny chickens and kids with naked asses in straw huts. You sat in your holes getting bored watching villagers watch you out of the corners of their Asian-slanted eyes as they went about their daily affairs. You felt a little strange intruding with automatic rifles, machine guns, mortars, and warplanes and heavy artillery on call while they ploughed barefooted with black water buffalo and squatted on the bare ground like monkeys, eating rice out of wooden bowls.

But then you got up and moved again to a place that looked exactly like the last place, but wasn't, and you dug in again. We knew, simply knew, that we were a colored pin on a map to some asshole in the rear. The asshole changed the color of our pin according to our fortunes or misfortunes—green meant we were lucky and safe, maybe back on

41

stand-down at Da Nang; yellow was if we boogied out on something; red meant danger; black signaled we were taking casualties. If an entire unit got lost or wiped out, we suspected the asshole simply removed the pin and threw it away and put another pin in its place. The pin moved an inch on the map, or a quarter-inch, and we got dutifully out of our holes and went and dug some more holes.

"I wish," said Frenchy, "zat someone would invent a portable hole zat you pick up and stuff in your packboard and carry around with you."

The sun baked your brain during the day until you could not think, and then the rains followed in the evening and made you stiff and wet and irritable. Sometimes the VC came at night and fired four or five times, then packed up and left until the next night, bored perhaps because it got where we didn't even bother to return fire half the time. Now and again we heard about some Marine in another platoon or company that got hit—one had been killed in Golf Company, we understood—but the war was so goddamned slow wherever we were that Sergeant Shireman said the VC objective was to bore us all to death and thus win the war.

Second Platoon set up at the Brick Piles for two or three days and watched peasants make bricks and rice farmers make rice. Dave Bruce and I hootched together again. Leslie broke out his camera and went around taking snapshots.

"That black-and-white or color?" O'Brien the Arab demanded when Leslie persuaded him to pose in front of his foxhole overlooking a rice paddy with water buffalo in the background.

"It's black-and-white."

O'Brien went into a false tantrum. "Jee-suz Kee-rist, Leslie. I'm white. You need some black in the picture. Hey, hey, Edgerton. We need some black in this picture. Get your splib ass over here."

Armed Forces Radio Service brought home to the foxhole through the magic of the transistor radio:

Little GTO . . . you know ya look real fine . . .

"Real, real fine, now sing about some *girls,*" Smitty said, jiving down the line, shirt off, snapping his fingers to the music.

I propped my feet up on a sandbag, lay my rifle across my chest, closed my eyes, and let the radio transport me back to cruising the strip, working on my car, and chasing girls. Hey, I was nineteen years old; cruising, working on your car, and chasing women was the good life.

Sergeant Shireman came down the line.

"Turn that shit down," he roared. "You wanna give our position away to every gook this side of the river?"

I opened one eye. "Every gook in Vietnam can *see* us here," I said.

"Yeah? Well, we ain't gonna entertain 'em."

It was Balla's radio. He got up and turned it down. My one open eye fell on the canal flowing by immediately to our front. I opened the other eye. Any kind of entertainment was at a premium in the foxholes. You could only ding so many dragonflies with rubber bands, tell so many lies about pussy, and, in my case, read Kipling so many times. I already knew all Kipling's poems by heart.

The longer I looked at the canal, the cleaner and cooler the water looked and the hotter and dirtier I felt. I sat up where I could see green plants waving in the current at the bottom of the canal.

"Hey, O'Brien. Feel like a douche?"

O'Brien studied the water. The sides of the canal were steep and grown over with foliage, but a narrow wooden footbridge spanned it. Dum-Dum Duminski joined us on the bridge. We called him Dum-Dum not because he was dumb but because, like a dum-dum bullet, once you fired him on a particular trajectory he was hard to stop. Someone said that was the Pollack in him. He didn't look Polish; he looked Italian.

"I ain't wading in that crap," Dum-Dum said, unfired by the thought.

"Grab my ankles, " I instructed.

I stripped off my utility shirt and the two of them, each

43

grasping an ankle, dunked me head down over the side of the bridge. I held my breath until I thought they weren't going to pull me back up—I could feel O'Brien chuckling. I came up sputtering and coughing with a disgusting glob of slimy greenish muck stuck to the center of my chest. I tried to flick it off. Then I grabbed it and tried to pull it off. It stretched like rubber.

"Jee-suz Kee-rist," O'Brien said, eyes magnified like saucers behind his glasses.

Those weren't green plants waving so delightfully in the current at the bottom of the canal. They were leeches. You could get them off you with C-rat salt or a lighted cigarette, but the anticoagulant they injected made you bleed profusely.

"Hey, Sergeant Shireman. What do you do for a sucking chest wound?" I yelled, bleeding.

He was folding up a poncho. He glanced up. "What the hell happened to you, Roberts?"

"How about a medal? I took an AK round in the chest and saved O'Brien's life. I saw the bullet coming for O'Brien and I jumped up and caught it myself."

The sergeant snorted. "O'Brien, go tell that gook sniper it's three shots for the price of one. Maybe he can still get all three of you."

One day word came down for all the automatic riflemen to report to the company CP, where the gunnery sergeant issued each of us a rifle sniper scope with an infrared lamp so you could see to shoot in the dark. What would Western technology think of next?

"You automatic riflemen were selected to be night snipers because you're the only ones with bipods on your weapons," the gunny explained. "Sight 'em in and get to work. The skipper wants some surprised gooks when they come sneaking up. He wants 'em surprised *tonight*."

The war was getting *serious*.

Peering through the scope at night gave everything a fluid green look, but you could see quite well through it for about two hundred meters with new batteries and a good infrared lamp. I sighted in on a cemetery to my front, as it seemed a likely place to surprise a VC. The cemetery was a jumble of small Buddhist shrines and statues surrounded by a fence. I waited, pulling two hour shifts with another AR man from First Platoon.

It seemed I had barely gotten to sleep on my two hours off when I felt a nudge. It was the second night of the sniper experiment.

"Anything?" I asked, yawning.

"Yeah. Two water bufs, an elephant, and a fuck-you lizard in a treetop," the comedian sang off-key.

He curled up in the hole and went to sleep while I flipped on the scope lamp and scanned the cemetery. I could see the Buddhist markings in the graveyard in the greenish cast. I turned the scope off and waited, scanning again every few minutes.

After an hour, I was stifling entire series of yawns. I stretched, trying to keep awake, and flipped on the infrared for about the fiftieth time. The pale green light in the scope passed across the cemetery. I searched my entire front, sector by sector, methodically, then started sweeping back.

Suddenly, I tensed. There was a man out there now where a moment ago there had been nothing. He was standing in the graveyard leaning almost nonchalantly against a tombstone, confident the night would hide him. His image appeared fuzzy and fluid in the glass, but I centered the white dot sight on the man's chest and watched him. He wore black pajamas, as did most peasants and VC. I clicked off the safety and my finger sneaked to the trigger. It was like the first day of buck season and you had this big godawful deer in your sights but you couldn't tell whether or not it had antlers. Orders were we didn't ding anybody until we spotted a weapon.

Then I spotted antlers. The man lifted a rifle from behind the tombstone and pointed it toward our lines. I beat him to it by squeezing off a three-round burst. The edge of the tombstone next to him exploded. The gook dropped to the ground like the Brick Piles had fallen on him.

I recovered from recoil in time to catch the VC getting back up. Before I could sight in for a second burst, he cast a bewildered look around, then took off running like one of his long-dead ancestors was after him. I was too surprised to react. What the hell was going on? Sergeant Shireman proved you could kill them, at least in the daytime, but at night they kept getting up and running off.

Someone popped a parachute flare. Ghostly shadows swept across the rice paddies and the cemetery beneath the miniature sun.

"I got him," I said, puzzled. "I got him—but he got up and ran off."

"Roberts, you fucking missed," said Sergeant Shireman. "I'm gonna send you back to the range."

The asshole with the map moved our pin and, like mushrooms, kept in the dark and fed horse shit, we pulled back from the Brick Piles and set up in our original positions at Duong Son. We didn't even have to dig new holes, which pleased Frenchy especially. Dave Bruce and I occupied our hole overlooking the spot where the banana tree used to be.

"One night," I confided to O'Brien, "I'm going to get one of them bastards."

Frustration had set in.

O'Brien grinned bright against his swarthy skin. "Whatcha gonna do with him, Roberts, if you get him—mount him on your wall?"

There was a hut to our right, a haystack in front of us with a vegetable garden behind it, and, since there was a full moon, the wide trail that came out of the bamboo tree line and entered the ville stood out like a silver ribbon. We had settled back into a familiar night routine of fifty percent alert. On my turn awake, I spotted a figure walking toward us on the path. By this time I had relinquished the sniper scope to someone else, but the moon was so bright I could detect the black sweat band around the gook's head. Shadows obscured the lower half of his body. I nudged Bruce awake.

"Gook out front," I whispered.

The team leader rustled around in the bottom of the hole to take a look. Not only did he never get tired, he never got excited either.

"Keep an eye on him," Bruce said. "It's probably just a villager out taking a shit."

With only a peep sight at night, it's tough to lock firmly into a target. About the best you can do is aim down the barrel and hope for the best. I kept my barrel on the gook as he came along the path and then stepped into shadows cast by the bamboo. Moonlight flitting through the leafy tops of the stalks kept him partially illuminated.

"If you're VC," I muttered, "you are one dead sonofabitch."

I was expecting it, so it did not catch me by surprise when the gook suddenly raised a rifle from the shadows. He fired almost immediately toward a position to my left where Lieutenant Rowe and Sergeant Shireman had emplaced a 3.5 rocket-launcher crew.

"Gotcha!" I shouted triumphantly, and squeezed off full automatic. Red tracers like furious bees streaked into the sniper's chest and kept going out his back, impaling him on a fluid spit. He went down. I knew he was down to stay.

Illumination exploded in the sky, which was standard operating procedure. I watched shadows of bamboo and shrubs drift across the place where my VC fell. He was not getting back up.

"Bruce, *this* time . . . let's go out there and get him."

I *would* mount him for O'Brien if that was what it took.

"You know the orders," Bruce said. "We don't leave our holes for any reason."

"He won't be there in the morning if I don't go get him now."

Bruce had a cool head. He wouldn't be swayed when he had his orders.

"You're staying right where you are 'til dawn, Roberts,"

he said. "There's probably a bunch more out there waiting for you. Remember the wiremen?"

Unconvinced, I still had no recourse but to wait. Unable to sleep because of the excitement and the suspicion that if I slept the VC's buddies would drag his body away like they had the time I set the TNT booby trap. I kept personal guard for the rest of the night. About an hour before dawn I thought I heard rustling in the bushes and was tempted to spray the bamboo with lead to keep the body draggers away. But then it was quiet again. The eastern sky began to turn purple and orange, and soon I could see individual bamboo growth. A Vietnamese boy came out of a hut and urinated against the wall.

"Okay," Bruce said.

I crept down the path with my weapon ready while Bruce covered me.

It was just like at the banana tree. I found spent .30 caliber cartridge casings, bits of coarse black cloth, and splatters of blood in drag marks through the bamboo.

There was one consolation. The VC at night might be ghosts, but at least they bled.

# Chapter 6

It WAS GOING to be a good day for the VC. None of us was ever going to forget Cam Ne.

I kept wading forward through rice field water so warm it felt like a bath taken with your clothes on, hoisting high my M-14 to keep it dry. The darkness that is most dark before dawn closed around our heads, while the even darker water closed, lapping like wet tongues, around our waists. Second Battalion was moving forward to sweep Cam Ne. The rice that by now had grown head tall was so thick that even had the sun been up, the war would still have focused down to just me and one or two others moving close on my flanks. Frenchy and O'Brien or maybe Yates. I could hear them, but I could not see them. It made you feel alone.

I picked up the pace, hoping I was still on line. You did not want to be left behind in Indian country. Not after the wiremen.

A sweep of Cam Ne two weeks before by Delta Company of the Second had become famous when Delta took small arms and automatic rifle fire from the village and subsequently discovered an extensive tunnel complex and firing positions in the floors of huts. A CBS television crew showed none of that; what it ran through America's living rooms instead was a film clip of a Marine setting fire to the roof of a hut with Morley Safer narrating: "If there were any Viet Cong in the hamlets, they were long gone."

Holding real estate was not part of a guerrilla's war, but battalion intel supposedly had word that the VC had moved back in as soon as Delta moved out. If we caught the Viet Cong by surprise, went the thinking, they'd have to stand up and fight.

It was hard for a battalion of Marines in full combat gear wading through rice paddies in the dark to take anyone or anything by surprise.

Reaching the perimeter path that circled the village, Second Battalion Marines rose out of the primordial muck. A crack of light was beginning to widen low along the eastern horizon, silhouetting briefly the heavily laden warriors who passed in front of it. It would soon be daylight. Someone ordered the pace picked up. We hurried along the wide path, strung out and moving, but cautious.

The pace slowed again after a Marine stepped into a punji pit. The point men began probing the way ahead with fixed bayonets. The wounded man was from my platoon. Our corpsman, "Doc" Lindstrom, knelt next to him, working on a boardful of rusty steel barbs sticking completely through the grunt's boot and foot. The pink dawn illuminated pain in the guy's face, but he bit his lip until it bled to keep from crying out. He would have to wait until after the sweep on the village started before Medevac choppers could come for him.

Lieutenant Rowe paused to whisper, "Doc, patch him up quick and leave somebody with him. We may need you later."

I hoped our pin on the map wasn't black.

The sun came up, as Kipling said, "like thunder outer China 'crost the Bay!" It illuminated bamboo poles stuck into the edges of the dike along the top of which the trail ran. Attached to the tops of the poles were *crossbows* rigged to fire by trip wires. The arrows pointed downtrail toward us, but the crossbows had been there so long that the bows had warped in the cocked position and would not fire.

It was full daylight by the time the companies and platoons of the Second staged outside Cam Ne, in the quiet of a morning disturbed only by the sounds of men and arms, and launched the sweep. No sounds came from the hamlet; it was as though everyone were still asleep. Everyone and everything. Chickens, pigs, water boos. Even the birds remained silent. It reminded me of one of those jungle movies where one guy says, "I don't like it, it's quiet." And the other guy says, "Yeah—too quiet."

The traditional bamboo fence held the village captive. Some type of Chinese mine booby trap had been attached to the gate where Second Platoon would enter. A booby trap could be neutralized by attaching a small amount of C-4 explosive or TNT to it and discharging it in place or it could be "dragged" by knotting a long line to the device and making it explode harmlessly by jerking it out of its place.

We dragged this one while the lead elements of the platoon crouched in a ditch and Smitty yanked on the line. The mine went off with a loud *whump!* that showered dirt and bamboo leaves. The platoon poured through the gate and spread out again across a front. The village had been evacuated. A couple of pigs and a water boo wandered around looking like they had not eaten in several days—but there were no people. Not even a single old crone sitting in front of her hut chewing betel nut. So much for the element of surprise.

Living fences of thorny bamboo generally sectioned off Vietnamese villages into smaller plots and gave advantage to the VC by breaking up large bodies of troops into small clusters of men which lost sight of and contact with each other. It was better for the VC, when they fought, to take on four or five men than to challenge an entire platoon or company. Knowing this, Marines moved cautiously through Cam Ne searching huts and bunkers and tunnel mazes, peering into rice urns, boxes, and deserted animal pens, finding little other than some VC propaganda and a few scattered items of clothing left behind when the occupants fled.

Puzzled, feeling the weight of the silence like the rest of us, Frenchy looked around and shrugged. "They even took their ancestors with them," he said.

By early afternoon, the bewildered battalion, expecting combat but finding *this,* dribbled out the far side of the settlement in squads and platoons. The VC had dug a fighting trench partially around the perimeter on this side of the village. The trench was about eighteen inches wide and two feet deep. A low dried-out fence of bamboo and thorns partially concealed the breastworks from the front. Ahead, about three hundred meters on the other side of a network of rice paddies, were another tree line and a smaller village, part of the Cam Ne complex. We could see nothing moving in the other village either.

Hotel Company fell out at the trench for a break while we waited for the rest of the battalion to catch up. O'Brien and Pete Yates displayed ARVN uniforms they found buried in the trees behind the trench. Finding the uniforms added credence to rumors we had been hearing about supposedly loyal government forces in the area having gone turncoat over to the VC. It was a helluva war when the troops you fought with today might be fighting against you tomorrow. Our ARVN interpretors made a big show of angrily condemning the turncoats, more to convince us of their own loyalty, we suspected, than out of genuine outrage.

Whoever the enemy was at Cam Ne, however, VC or ARVN traitors, they had apparently gone, taking the population with them. Hotel shed flak jackets and packs. Marines drew water out of wells and, with a great deal of grab-assing and relieved laughter, dumped bucketfuls over each other's heads. A skinny chicken came squawking fast-legged out of a bamboo thicket pursued by a gleeful-eyed Sergeant Shireman with his .45 pistol in one hand and a knife in the other. We had eaten nothing since the day before. Sergeant Shireman was apparently intent on having something other than canned Cs for chow, for, a few minutes later, he came back chasing a piglet he found hiding inside a hut. The platoon cheered him on as the squealing pig, kicking up a tiny trail of dust ahead of the tall Marine, zigzagged among the dodging, shouting grunts. Lieutenant Rowe, keeping his distance, grinned shyly and shook his head.

Things settled down after a few minutes and even Sergeant Shireman, losing his races with both the chicken and the pig—"Cocksuckers're faster'n they look"—settled for a cold meal of Cs. Sitting with my legs dangling inside the VC trench, I glanced up from a can of lima beans and ham to find one of the company interpreters grinning down at me. His name was Tran Hoa.

*"Como tally vous?"* I never missed a chance to practice my high-school French. Tran had fought with the French against the Viet Minh. "What're you doing here?"

The ARVN slapped me on the shoulder and giggled like a schoolgirl. My accent never failed to amuse and delight him. He replied in the pidgin English Vietnamese and Americans commonly used in communicating with each other.

"Come see numbah ten Cam Ne," he said. "Kill beaucoup VC same-same Marine." He laughed.

O'Brien was mining his own can of Cs nearby. "No beaucoup VC," he interjected. "Beaucoup bullshit."

Tran Hoa stopped giggling. The lines of age and hardship engraved in his face visibly deepened as he squinted in the sun at the other village across the rice paddies from us, as though he saw something there none of the rest of us had. I took another look to make sure. Quiet. Yeah—*too* quiet.

Tran pointed, aiming down his point. "Beaucoup VC here," he predicted.

"Dinky dow old bastard," O'Brien grumbled, but he took another look, too.

"You see, you see," the ARVN said, then walked off in the direction of the company CP back in the trees.

So far, we had been fighting ghosts who came out fleetingly only at night. Most of us had given up in contempt the hope of ever having a *real* fight in the daylight with the little men in black. They were gutless little bastards who sneaked around trying to cut off a Marine or two in order to torture them and string them up in trees. Unknown to us, however, we were about to pay a price for getting slack. Afterward, I could imagine how we must have looked to the VC hiding in the opposite tree line—like a bunch of rear-echelon pogues grab-assing and hooting and pouring water over our heads and lying around eating in the open and chasing pigs and chickens. We hadn't yet learned to respect the VC.

A quiet blond kid from First Platoon was the first to pay the price for our carelessness. Like me, he was sitting on the side of the VC trench, legs inside, drinking from a canteen. Suddenly, before the report of the shot carried across the rice paddies, a startled look crossed his face and his canteen fell from his hands. The sound of the shot, a flat crack, followed, and the kid toppled slowly over to one side—dead. The slug took him dead center in the chest between the gap of his flak jacket. The jacket wouldn't have stopped it anyhow.

A volley of gunshots chorused across the rice paddies. A corporal named Oller jumped up. A bullet shattered his arm at the elbow and spun him completely around in his tracks before he dropped. He screamed.

Pandemonium erupted. Everyone was trying to get into the trench at the same time. A VC in the other village fast-tracked from one bush to another. He stopped and aimed his AK. He fired and a black machine gunner running toward the trench with his M-60 did an acrobatic flip in the air. His gun went sailing. He landed on his back. His mouth gulped like a fish's once or twice and one leg jerked. Then blood gushed out his fish's mouth and he died.

Cries of "Corpsman! Corpsman!" filled the suddenly deadly air. I saw lanky Doc Lindstrom, heedless of the bullets flying, rushing from one downed Marine to another before I tumbled into the trench and frantically thrust my M-14 on bipods above the lip of the trench and blindly squeezed off a couple of bursts at a small temple I could see outlined in the opposing bamboo.

When a bullet passes near your head, it makes a cracking sound that seems to steal all the air around you. Astonished at the VC's audacity in attacking a full company of Marines in the sunshine, I helped pour fire across the rice at the opposite bamboo, laying down a field of fire to gain fire superiority. I heard the cracking sounds all around me as red tracers and enemy green tracers plunged in brilliant lines across the open field.

Nothing before this—the snipings, the endless sweeps, the searches—had been combat. This was classic combat. For the first time we were actually catching glimpses of the enemy standing up to fight us in the daylight.

I spotted a figure jump up foolishly and run along a dike. I swiveled my rifle on its bipod, caught the gook in my sights, and squeezed off. Matilda waltzed. The figure tumbled behind the dike. I couldn't tell if I had hit him or he had decided to get his ass down and buttoned up. I waited, but he did not reappear.

ONTOS—tracked tank killers—had accompanied the battalion sweep in case of reinforced bunkers. One of them rolled up on line, snarling and growling, like a giant green insect out of some Saturday afternoon horror flick, and opened up with the deep *cough!* of its .50-caliber spotter rifle. The tracer streamed into the temple, making a crunching sound as it struck the stone. Then the ONTOS fired its 106mm recoilless rifle. One wall of the temple disintegrated. Smoke wreathed into the clear sky.

The sounds of battle were deafening, like hiding under a piece of tin during a hail storm.

It was Sergeant Shireman's day. He was everywhere, skittering up and down the line directing fire, adding words of encouragement here and there. He must live a charmed life. Even with all the lead flying, he remained unscathed, the strap of his helmet flying, the half grin stuck on his face as he paused now and again in full sight to crank off a couple of rounds at the enemy. It awed the rest of us. "Ain't no bullet in the world can get near Sergeant Shireman," we began telling each other, and believing it. The man was invincible.

I watched an artillery FO creeping around in the tall rice forward of us, his radio antenna sticking into the air to pinpoint his movement. I couldn't figure what the fool was doing, unless he thought Forward Observer meant he had to be forward of the line of combat. I learned later he was a new lieutenant, a boot like the rest of us, on his first combat mission, and that he was assigned by battalion to direct artillery fire in case we needed it.

We needed it. Sergeant Shireman came tearing along the trench behind us.

"Grab your pots," he yelled as he ran, hunched over. "Get your flak jackets on. We're calling in artillery."

The boot lieutenant was radioing a 105 howitzer battery located across the river from us for a fire mission. What we did not know was that in his excitement the boot gave the battery *our* grid coordinates instead of the enemy's and that, instead of asking for an adjustment round, he demanded an immediate "Fire for effect."

That meant the battery opened up with everything it had. We were about to experience what was known as "friendly fire." Green as I was, I knew something was wrong when I heard the big shells coming, sounding something like Volkswagens being hurled through the air. They were coming in too low, dropping.

On us.

Ironically enough, the boot lieutenant responsible for the mistake got zapped first. An air burst directly over his head flattened him out in the rice. Thirty-two more 105 shells walked up and down our lines, pulverizing everything in their path, shaking up a cloud of dust and smoke that, from the vicinity of the airbase, must have looked like a storm cloud on the horizon.

The earth exploded around me, and kept exploding. Shrapnel screamed through the air, cutting it. Clods of dirt and rock pelted out of the sky like blocks of ice.

I dug my face into the dirt at the bottom of the trench and

held on lest the earth hurtle me off into space. Its having occurred to me that my hands clasped on top of my head might get blown off, I rammed both inside my helmet and grabbed the webbing and hung on again.

The shelling lasted for what had to be an eternity. Then it stopped as abruptly as it began and the ensuing silence was so profound that the ringing in my ears was as horrible as the shelling itself. After awhile, still eating dirt, I heard the first plaintive moans and startled cries of "Corpsman! Corpsman!" I knew Doc Lindstrom would be out there. I wondered if he had been out there all through it.

Shaken and spent by the fury I had endured, I crawled tentatively over the edge of the trench to take a look. I could only stare. Ten minutes ago, when Sergeant Shireman was chasing the chicken, was a lifetime past. Now, the earth had gone through an upheaval; it had been ploughed and cratered and furrowed. It was a scene from Hades—wounded and dying Marines lying everywhere like grotesque storefront dummies with arms and legs and other pieces broken off, among which, slowly, still in shock, Marines still whole were beginning to walk to look for the faces of their buddies, unmindful of whether or not the enemy was still firing.

Fortunately, the enemy was not. Our own artillery had done their job for them, and far more effectively.

A corporal named Wiseman had sought cover with George Renninger. A shell blew him out of the hole, like lifting up a rag doll and throwing it away. Renninger remained unscathed and had started out in the storm of steel and smoke to rescue his friend.

"No!" Wiseman screamed, lying in the open but reaching back with palms wide and fingers splayed. "Don't get out! Stay put. It'll kill you!"

A moment later, a second detonating round picked Wiseman off the ground and flung him through the bamboo thorn fence, ripping off his right arm. As soon as the shelling stopped, some Marines, Doc Lindstrom among them, ran by carrying Wiseman in a poncho. The poncho was full of blood. I couldn't tell if they had Wiseman's arm in the poncho with him or not.

Half of Hotel Company suffered at least minor wounds. It took three H-34 Medevac choppers to load up the casualties and fly them out. Tran Hoa picked up my pack from where it had been blown twenty meters away.

"Ro'bear?" he asked. "This you?"

I dug a piece of shrapnel out of the mess kit inside. I held it clenched in my palm as the helicopters, loaded with bleeding and mangled Marines, rose from the heap that had been Hotel Company and beat up the sky for the second time that afternoon. Hotel Company was no longer unblood-ied and untried.

It had been a good day for the Viet Cong. Our pin on the map must have been black.

# Chapter 7

BACK WHEN WE LEFT Da Nang, crossing the Phong Le Bridge, it might not have *looked* any different on the other side, but we were finding out it *was* different. While that had only been weeks ago, it seemed like years.

"A man," Frenchy reflected in that way he had of getting to the heart of a matter, "he can get himself killed in zees war."

That one fact was being impressed upon us more and more frequently. Once, not so long ago in the optimism of youth I was quickly losing, I had thought I would live forever. Now, like Frenchy, I wasn't so sure anymore.

The week before Cam Ne, Lieutenant Regan, weapons platoon leader, got it. Stateside, he had been a prick who would storm into his platoon's bay in the middle of the night to hold barracks inspection, or would have his men up marching for some real or imagined infraction of an obscure rule. He demanded discipline, he said, discipline, discipline, discipline—spotless spit-shined boots, creased uniforms, military courtesies and respect without fail. Spit-shined boots, he said, was the way to win wars because it instilled in men the discipline to endure hardships and deprivations.

You can have discipline without being a prick. He was a prick.

In Vietnam, he started to change. He was finding out wars weren't fought in spit-shined boots after all, that men fought and died for a variety of reasons, chief among them loyalty and respect and, yes, *love* for one another. Lieutenant Regan was finding out that he needed his men more than they needed him in order to stay alive, and that, in war, a prick could be amputated. He started to change, but he didn't have that much time.

"He was an asshole," someone remarked after the fact, "but he didn't stink as bad as he used to."

A sniper got him on a company sweep through a rice field outside a ville called Giang Dong. The lieutenant was one man back from point, followed by his radioman. Snipers were able to pick out the officers because of the radio antennas that followed them around. Platoon lieutenants had a high casualty rate in Vietnam.

A single shot echoed across the flooded field. Lieutenant Regan jerked once, as though from an invisible line on his heart. He plunged forward into the green shoots, dead instantly.

A second shot immediately after the first caught one of the ammo bearers named Gonzales through both calves and sent him down thrashing in the rice.

Usually a sniper fired at most two or three times before fading away to try his luck later. This one did not have that chance. Someone spotted his muzzle flashes and smoke and pinpointed his hiding place with a burst of red tracers. Tracers from the entire company front apex'd in on the luckless gook. He kept running from one place to another, chased by the tracers. It was something like chasing a mouse in a cornfield.

Lance Corporal Alfred Ekstein airbursted a grenade from a launcher over the VC's last hiding place at the edge of the village. The gook jumped up to run again, with his black pajamas leaving a contrail of smoke from the white phosphorus. The black machine gunner who was to be killed at Cam Ne made the gook do a jerky little dance, like a puppet gone mad on a string.

The company cheered wildly.

That was last week. This week it was Cam Ne and the blond kid was dead and the black machine gunner. Oller had been wounded, Wiseman lost an arm and was maybe dead, too, and a bunch of others was missing from our ranks due to friendly fire.

How could you call any fire *friendly* that was killing you?

I noticed something about Frenchy I hadn't noticed before.

"Frenchy, you look *old*, man." He was no older than I.

"It ees zee maturity of war," he said.

The battalion cleared out the village—part of Cam Ne—from which we had taken the killing fire. It turned out to be a maze of underground passageways and tunnels connecting a fighting network of hootches, spider traps, and other defensive positions. We attacked a position where there were muzzle flashes only to find the occupant gone by way of an escape tunnel. We swept through an area, clearing it, only to be shot at from behind. Drop a grenade into a tunnel and five minutes later some gook was back in the same tunnel firing us up, inflicting casualties.

We kept the air filled over Cam Ne with Medevac helicopters.

Up until now, Marines had been using CS grenades—tear gas—to run gooks out of their holes. That way you didn't kill the women and kids; the tear gas was effective but harmless. However, after Hanoi and Peking railed against the use of "gas" by American troops, calling it "inhumane," our own news media stateside overreacted and headlines screamed with charges of "chemical warfare."

The tear gas was taken away from us and we got smoke. Smoke was more effective than tear gas, the way we learned to use it, and much more deadly. Not the smoke grenades themselves. The fires. What we did was toss a smoke down a tunnel and cover the opening with a poncho to let the smoke seep out of other exits that might have gone undetected. With troops then stationed at every escape point, we covered all the air holes with ponchos and poured gasoline into the underground passages. After the fumes had had time to seep into every corner and pocket of the tunnel, a grenade or trip flare ignited everything underground and made it an active volcano.

It seemed it was okay to turn the VC into crispy critters but not to make them cry.

Because of the friendly fire and the fighting before and afterward, Hotel Company suffered the most and was being rotated back to the airbase for rest and refitting. Slogging wearily along in a scattered line, leaving the village complexes of Cam Ne, some of us turned to look back. Curling columns of black smoke wisped up over the tree line from the village.

"Christmas," said Frenchy with a sigh. "She may never come to Vietnam."

# Chapter 8

A FEW NIGHTS BEFORE Hotel Company passed back across the Phong Le Bridge to "safe" country, a handful of suicidal Viet Cong attacked the airbase and burned one Skyhawk and damaged two others. The sun burned brightly down upon the blackened hulk that had been dragged off the asphalt apron and left in the dirt. As we trooped by, looking considerably more seasoned than when we left mere weeks before, every eye in the company fell upon the destroyed airplane. It was almost like we had been individually violated in our own bedrooms. It proved that in this war there was no such place as a "safe" area.

The company set up near the airfield just behind the outer perimeter. Lieutenant Rowe posted the platoon's own security—just in case—while the rest of us stripped for real showers set up in tents.

"All of Vietnam," Frenchy said, "we will never get washed off."

* * *

There was a lot of down time that spawned and cultured rumors among the mushrooms. There were rumors of massive escalations and big operations, of being extended in Vietnam (this was before the one-year individual tours), and of Russian supply and troop ships entering Haiphong Harbor in the north. The rear echelon pogues, back where they could get all the juicy gossip, fed us more rumors about corruption and pending coups in the South Vietnamese government. They said if that happened, we might have to pull out fast.

The rumors we liked best, which were widely and eagerly circulated and which were probably the least founded of any of the rumors, had to do with R & R—rest and relaxation, "rape and ruin," "sex and sin." The rumors kept proliferating, although we remained stuck on the airbase like squatters waiting to harvest crops that had never been planted.

"Roberts, what would your Kipling say?" O'Brien asked.

"About what?"

"Did all he ever do was go out and fight with Gunga Din and all that—or did he have some fun, too?"

I laughed. "Hey, O'B-san, ol' Rudyard had an eye for the ladies."

"Oh, yeah? You mean all them old guys back then actually went out and—*fucked?*"

"Listen to this."

I started reading him *The Ladies:*

> I've taken my fun where I've found it;
> I've rouged an' I've ranged in my time;
> I've 'ad my pickin' o' sweethearts,
> An' four o' the lot was prime.

From then on, as long as we were at the airbase among the rumors that never panned out, O'Brien or Frenchy or Smitty—sometimes even Bruce—would sidle up to me on an idle afternoon.

"How about the ladies?"

"What about the ladies?"

"Read that Kipling guy who wasn't no pansy. Read about the ladies."

Afterward, O'Brien would say, "That's what I want, just like Kipling said—'A tiddy live 'eathan—a doll in a teacup.' And I'll fuck her before Cs and I'll fuck her . . ."

"Where will you keep her?" Frenchy wanted to know, entering the fantasy.

"In my pack, you dumb fuck. Where else?"

"You would have to get rid of your mess kit."

O'Brien's dark Arab eyes gleamed. "I wouldn't need it anymore. I'd just eat pussy."

"You white boys is weird," Edgerton said.

"O'Brien ain't white," I said. "He's brown. He's a splib like you."

"He eat pussy, he a white boy."

Part of being in "the rear" was taking care of the admin and medical details that had a way of getting neglected in the field. Sergeant Shireman sent me over to company to pick up my health records. I was supposed to see the dentist.

The dentist's office was located in a GP-medium spread next to an 81mm mortar pit. Every time the mortars went off in response to a fire mission request from across the river, whichever unfortunate leatherneck happened to be confined in the dentist's torture rack with his mouth open damned near leaped out of his hide.

The doctor took my file and hummed happily while he studied it.

"Private Roberts, you notice my neighbors are mortars?" he asked.

"Yes, sir."

"Sometimes they fire them."

"Yes, sir."

"You don't bite me when they do and I don't perform any unnecessary surgery."

A helluva deal. "Yes, sir."

"Looks like you have two more wisdom teeth to come out," he said.

"I had two cut out already in boot camp."

"Well, there are two more on the bottom. Don't worry. We'll get them."

I climbed gingerly into the wooden field dental chair. I would rather have been crawling down spider holes after gooks. The doctor swung a dim light over my face. The light throbbed from the generator chugging away outside.

"Okay, I'm going to make an incision. It may hurt a little."

"Uh, Doc?"

"Yeah?"

"You didn't give me an anesthetic."

"Sorry. You should have been here yesterday. We still had some Novocaine left."

He propped my mouth open with a clamp and started to work while my eyes rolled and my knuckles turned white on the chair handles.

"You Marines are tough," he said, probing in my mouth. "You can take it. . . ."

We had thought the incessant sun was bad. The rains were worse as the monsoon season tumbled around on every evening's horizon. You packed everything you owned, trying to keep it dry, and it mildewed in your pack overnight. Your feet in their boots wrinkled up and turned white like used soap and started to rot. You got soaked and then the sun came out again and you stewed in your juices. And so we waited some more in the rain. Kept in the dark and fed horse shit. It was better across the river than sitting here like mushrooms while rumors kept spreading.

O'Brien's unremitting good humor helped the squad keep some perspective. One morning I rolled out of my poncho, stiff and damp, awakened by a commotion outside the tent.

"Jee-suz Kee-rist! Roberts? Roberts? Talk to me, buddy," O'Brien wailed in falsetto, putting on an act. "Sombody get the lieutenant. Get Lloyd Bridges. Get Jacques Cousteau. Get the chaplain. We gotta get Roberts outa there."

The Arab was wringing his hands over my foxhole. The hole was full of muddy rainwater, on the surface of which floated my upside-down helmet with I KILL VC TO KEEP RITA FREE inscribed on the camouflage cover. Rita was my girl.

"Yates . . . Yates, goddamnit . . . Roberts has drowned," O'Brien continued dramatically. "We gotta have a burial at sea."

I walked up, yawning. O'Brien ignored me.

"O'B-san, I'm right here."

O'Brien pretended surprise. His eyes rolled owlishly behind his glasses. "Roberts! Thank God. For a minute there, buddy, I thought you was a goner."

"Not me, man. I loaned my helmet to Smitty last night."

"Oh, my God! Jee-suz Kee-rist! *Smitty? . . . Smitty?*"

Mail call was the highlight of every day. Along with the letters from wives and mothers and girlfriends came several editions of *Navy Times* and *Stars and Stripes*. The newspapers passed through the platoon like, as Pete Yates put it with his home-grown Ozark drawl, "salts through a goose." We were hungry for news about home, any news. Groups of Marines clumped to look over each other's shoulders. One day a larger-than-normal crowd gathered to mull over a front page picture of a California National Guardsman standing next to an 81mm mortar—on a street corner in Watts, a black section of Los Angeles where headlines said there had been racial rioting. People had been killed there in fiercer battles than some we were having in Vietnam.

That was also the first time we heard about "war protestors" at a place called Berkeley. Some students, the papers said, had had a sit-down strike across a railroad track to dramatize their opposition to the war in Vietnam. Stunned, O'Brien looked at the pictures for a minute, scratched his head, and said it for all of us:

"Jee-suz Kee-rist!"

Smitty squatted next to me and picked his teeth with a

weed stem. A farm boy from Missouri, Smitty was the largest man in the platoon, a cross between a work horse and a pack mule. On a mission he often ended up carrying extra ammo and supplies, but he took them cheerfully and was always asking if there was anything else he could do. He had a way of breaking life down to its simplest terms and then digesting it in bite-sized pieces.

I jabbed a finger at the newspapers and summed it up for the big man: "They're saying we're interfering with a civil war that ain't none of our business."

Smitty chewed on his weed and spat through his teeth.

"How the hell they know what's going on over here?" he said. "Ain't none of them college pukes ever been here."

That was how we referred to the war protestors—"college pukes." We came to resent them fiercely not so much for their opposition to the war as for the privilege they had of sitting safely back on their asses to protest while we were over here fighting the war for them. It boiled down to simple terms—they were against the war, they were against *us*. Bringing up the subject of war protestors always ignited a spirited session on what ought to be done with them.

"What they ought to do is send the bastards over for a little education Marine-style. Send them out on night listening posts."

"They'd have to go unarmed though, 'cause the spoiled little darlings wouldn't want to hurt anybody."

"Wonder how long it'd take 'em to change their minds once they started getting hung up by their heels with their guts cut open and their balls stuck in their mouths."

"Well, now, reckon that ain't never gonna happen. If they *had* any balls, they'd be over here now instead of whining and crying around in the newspapers."

Rain cut the conversation short. It reached one end of the tent city with a rapid drumming on canvas and swept toward us on line. We grabbed our helmets and rifles and ducked for cover. A copy of *Stars and Stripes* with the picture of the college pukes face up to the clouds lay on the ground.

Rain soaked it immediately; it melted to conform with the soil. That wasn't good enough. O'Brien dashed back and brought the heel of his combat boot down hard and ground the picture into the Vietnam mud.

He wore a satisfied grin when he came ducking out of the rain.

# Chapter 9

S ERGEANT SHIREMAN, something big's about to go down, huh? We a part of it or what?"

"Roberts, you are a goddamned fucking boot Marine," Sergeant Shireman said good-naturedly. "You'll be told what you're supposed to know when the time comes."

"Then it's true. They're going to move our pin. What color's the pin?"

"Red," said Sergeant Shireman, his hawk's eyes piercing.

Red meant danger.

That was one rumor that turned out to be founded. The battalion was going on a big operation. It was supposed to be code-named "Operation Satellite," but a clerk made an error and it became "Operation Starlight," the single most successful operation of the entire war if you looked at their body count and compared it to ours.

Reconnaissance and intel had discovered that the VC were using the Van Tounge Peninsula as a staging area, or jumping-off point, for attacks on the Da Nang airfield. That was how they had gotten in the last time to burn the Skyhawks.

The Third Marines found themselves launching a classical beach assault against fortified enemy positions on the southernmost coast of the peninsula, while companies from the Fourth and Seventh Marines were heli-lifted deep into the jungle to set up a blocking force.

Skyhawks and Phantoms using napalm and cannon fire, assisted by the Navy's offshore six-inch guns, pounded the center of the trap where more than two thousand crack North Vietnamese troops were trapped. The NVA fought back with a ferocity that must have surprised planners of the campaign, who were accustomed to the hit-and-run tactics of the guerrillas across the Phong Le Bridge.

Enemy body count exceeded six hundred. For hours after the battle, choppers flew continuously back to Da Nang laden with Marine dead and wounded. Corpses were stacked like cordwood in the backs of trucks, while bulldozers pushed dirt over big holes filled with the bodies of the enemy. There was a lab in Da Nang that worked around the clock stuffing Marines' bodies into black plastic bags and shipping them refrigerated back home to Mom.

Hotel Company, still understrength from having received no replacements, drew the light end of the operation with a diversionary sweep up the coast north of where the NVA were trapped. We were trucked to the coast and dropped off. ONTOS tank killers led the way, clattering up the beach next to the sea, carrying our packboards for us while the company followed walking in a long tactical march behind.

There was a break in the rains and it turned out mostly to be a walk in the sun. The sea lay bright and beautiful and quiet beneath a pale blue dome of sky. Stately palms rose above green foliage on the beach. The scene had everything except surf. The water came in and lapped timidly at the beach like a rich woman's poodle.

"No fucking surf!" I yelled at O'Brien the Arab. "How can civilized man live in a country with no surf?"

"What's the matter with you, Roberts, huh? This is serious shit, man. This is a *war*."

\* \* \*

At mid-morning, we cleared out and burned a field of anti-paratrooper punji stakes six feet tall. The poisoned bamboo stakes crackled in the fire and popped like AK rounds. Black smoke still climbed the air currents behind us as we came to a village set back in the trees from the sea. By now, bored with it all and a little disappointed that we had not been included in the main thrust of the operation—"a bridesmaid instead of a bride"—I fell carelessly into the squad line behind Dum-Dum Duminski and a kid named McNey, who was thin and sharp-featured and resembled a CPA or a mail clerk who had somehow mistakenly been assigned to a grunt line company.

The squad filed slowly along a trail leading to the village and came to the familiar bamboo gate. It was closed. Some kids and old women waited silently among the hootches and watched our advance. They did not move.

"Do you think," Frenchy asked, "that they know we are here to save them?"

"Nuke 'em all," Leslie said, "an' let God sort 'em out. They're just waiting to see us get zapped."

Duminski and McNey continued forward to the gate, wiping sweat. Instead of going with them, as I normally would, I paused on the trail, leaning on my rifle, and reached for my canteen. Warm Kool-Aid washed the dust from my throat.

Around the sides of the canteen I saw the two Marines examine the gate for sabotage. Apparently satisfied, McNey unlatched the wire catch and took a step out of the way to let the gate swing open.

There was a blinding flash of light and a muffled *carrump!* as the booby trap buried underneath the gate detonated. The two Marines became the nucleus of a geyser of dust, leaves, and black smoke. With a surprised scream, Duminski dropped his rifle and fell to his knees in the trail, clawing insanely at his eyes. I caught McNey in my arms as he reeled back. He was also grabbing for his eyes. I sat him down at the side of the trail while someone started yelling for Doc Lindstrom.

McNey was blubbering terror into his hands. "God, I'm blind! Oh, fuck, man, *my eyes . . .*" He started rocking back and forth, moaning, hands like live things on his powder-blackened face.

"Mac, you'll be all right," I tried to reassure him.

*"I'm fucking blind, man!"*

"Maybe not. Corpsman! Corpsman!"

*"I'm blind!"*

And maybe he was. I couldn't help thinking that it could just as easily have been me, too—if I hadn't stopped for a drink of Kool-Aid. Fortune was with me. Lady Luck. That Big Somebody up there was looking over me. Then I felt a tinge of guilt for being thankful that, if it had to be anyone, it was them instead of me.

Doc Lindstrom—all corpsman were called "Doc"—was on his way. I heard him running up the file with his aid bag. He was a tall, gangling, nearsighted sailor with thick glasses that made him look like he was peering through the ends of Coke bottles. The VC were starting to keep him busy. His practice was picking up. This time it had been a glass quart jar filled with rock, sand, broken glass, and gun powder.

As he started working on the casualties, I stood up slowly and let my eyes lift to beyond where the small crater continued to smoke at the gate. The women and kids around the hootches had vanished. They knew all along what was going to happen. As Leslie said, they were waiting to see it. They may even have set the trap for us. I experienced a moment of such intense hatred that it was all I could do to prevent Matilda from doing a waltz from one side of the village to the other.

"Roberts?"

It was Sergeant Shireman.

"Let it go, Roberts," he said.

The villagers kept prudently out of sight as we swept through, after a helicopter dust-off for Dum-Dum and McNey. We found several more booby traps. While farther down the peninsula Marines were making an assault against a "hot" beach and engaging in the kind of stand-up battle

73

for which we had been trained, here, for Hotel Company, it remained the same war of attrition. Trip wires, crossbows, punji pits, booby traps, snipers—*these* were the enemy—and silent villagers who impassively watched us take our lumps one or two at a time.

"Jee-suz Kee-rist!" O'Brien roared. "Why don't the bastards come out and fight?"

"Why should they?" I felt discouragement all the way to the soles of my aching feet. "They can get us easier like this without ever showing themselves."

In the evening Hotel Company dug in on a line stretching across the beach from the water to an old French concrete fort left over from when the Viet Cong were calling themselves Viet Minh and the French were doing the fighting. All during the afternoon jets had screamed back and forth overhead, racing from the airfield to dump bombs and napalm on the trapped NVA. We heard the constant distant rumble of their explosions and of the Navy shells landing on target. It sounded like a thunderstorm brewing just on the other side of the horizon. I half expected black clouds to appear, but the weather held, and by the time night fell the thunder had subsided.

"Hey, Frenchy," I called from the fighting hole I shared with Dave Bruce.

A shadow against new stars, Frenchy climbed out of his hole and ambled over to mine. He was smoking. Bruce disapproved of the red telltale dot in the dark, but he said nothing. After all, the VC and the NVA were too busy down the peninsula to concern themselves with us.

I pointed at the square shadow of the French fort. "Looks like your relatives built another bunker way out in the middle of nowhere to hide in."

"Not *my* relatives, my friend," he returned patiently. "I am French *Canadian*."

He studied the concrete monstrosity with its fields of fire commanding the beach.

"The French patrolled during zee day and hid inside their

bunkers in zee night," he said reflectively. "That ees why zee VC are used to fighting at night."

"Then we have them fooled, don't we?" I said.

"How ees that?"

I chuckled wearily. *"We* patrol both day and night."

"That ees *very* true," Frenchy admitted, reaching for his canteen.

And it was.

# Chapter 10

KIPLING HAD THE HEART AND SOUL of a grunt. He knew what it was like to be fucking malaria-wet miserable and still have to keep going, to prove what was deep inside, whether steel or simply a rusted strand of wire about to break. After a while, slogging the rice paddies and jungles, day after day, night after night, getting skinnier and sicker by the day from intestinal parasites and mosquitos and leeches and blisters and heat, harassed constantly by the deadly nagging of little men in black you seldom saw, just experienced, the grind of this kind of combat wore you down until, sometimes, you wanted to throw up your hands in surrender and yell at Ho Chi Minh: "Fuck you, Ho. Just get it over with!"

Home was a distant memory, a place you always remembered but often tried not to remember because of the hollow it left inside. Little things could summon such memories at unexpected times and places—something no more, say, than a bottle of perfume.

Following Operation Starlight, somebody moved our pin on the map and Second Platoon got transferred out of Hotel

Company, Second Battalion, to Mike Company, Third Battalion, which had taken over our old operations on the far side of the Phong Le Bridge. Mike, we were told, had lost one of its platoons in a U-shaped ambush and needed a replacement platoon. Second platoon was it.

"Jee-suz Kee-rist, buddies!" O'Brien exclaimed indignantly. "We are taking the place of dead men."

Sergeant Shireman just grinned in that hawkish way he had that could mean anything but generally meant he was having a pretty good time doing the job he had trained to do. He could grin if he wanted; Second had taken fewer casualties than any other platoon in Hotel. We were beginning to accredit Sergeant Shireman with that. And Lieutenant Rowe. The lieutenant was turning out pretty good. He knew when to let Sergeant Shireman run things.

"Saddle up, Marines," Sergeant Shireman ordered. "The war waits for nobody."

"That's wonderful," George Renninger decided, reading a letter from home. A slightly built kid, short and thin, he most often formed a quiet background for any gathering. "Call it off for lack of interest," he suggested gloomily, "and send me home—before I go in a box."

The firefight and friendly fire at Cam Ne had affected him somehow. When he did talk, he often talked about the bodies carried out in ponchos with blood streaming to the ground.

It was not difficult to saddle up and move when you could stuff all your possessions into a packboard or drape them on your body somewhere. Uncomfortable, yes—war is *never* comfortable—but not difficult. Second Platoon of Hotel 2/9 became Second Platoon of Mike 3/9 by the simple process of loading into a six-by on top of a bed of sandbags—the sandbags were in case the truck ran over a mine—trucking through the slums of Da Nang we called "Dog Patch," and crossing the Phong Le Bridge to where the Third Battalion was set up around Giang Dong.

"I ain't never gonna cross any more bridges when I leave this fucking place," Renninger declared. "Something bad starts happening every time we cross the sonofabitch."

77

Rain started to dribble out of lowering clouds as we rushed through the squalor and overcrowding of Dog Patch and turned onto the open road, escorted by gun jeeps. I hunkered down in the open truck between Smitty and O'Brien, trying to use my flak jacket for walls and my helmet as a roof. Water dripped steadily off the edges of the helmet.

Rita had sent me a bottle of perfume. A little whiff of it and I was instantly back home. Just like that. With her under one arm on a Saturday night. It did miracles for me even a bottle of Tiger Piss could not equal.

It even made the rain go away.

I fished for it in my utility pocket and, removing the cap carefully so as not to spill any, took a deep hit of the fragrance. Smitty sniffed suspiciously. Sharing, I passed the bottle to him.

"Rita's," I explained with a sheepish grin. "It's so I don't forget how girls are supposed to smell back home."

The giant's eyes bugged. "Oh, man. That's the only thing I've smelled in this country that don't stink."

The truckload of wet, bedraggled Marines came alive.

"Get off your ass. Pass it around."

They sniffed and moaned. It worked the same magic for them that it did for me.

O'Brien's eyes twinkled mischievously behind their black frames. "Roberts, are you sure this ain't yours?"

"You'll never know, sailor," I lisped.

On the perimeter at Giang Dong, the harassed-looking commander of Mike Company greeted us, wiping his face with a filthy green rag. We stood around leaning on our rifles and watching the strangers lolling in their holes among the bamboo. The captain's welcome fell far short of the rousing one given by Lieutenant Rowe when he took over the platoon at Pendleton.

"Welcome to Mike Company, Third Battalion," he said hurriedly. "Lieutenant Rowe tells me you've been here before. The gunny will show you where to set up in the perimeter. Do your job as Marines and we'll get along fine."

That was all. The platoon dug in on the edge of the village

looking west toward a swelling of bluish mountains rising from the interior. A contingent of "Popular Forces" from the village defense force was on the perimeter with us. Two of the "Ruff Puffs," as we called them, were assigned a position with me. While I labored over digging my hole—just deep enough to sit on the edge and hang my legs into it (we had given up the deep holes)—the Ruff Puffs watched with amusement, jabbering to each other. Although it had been raining, the ground was still hard and rocky.

Presently, the Ruff Puffs strung hammocks in the bamboo behind me and crawled into them for naps. No worries. The Marines were here to protect them.

I finished the hole just before dark. Scraping clay into a mound parapet in front of it, I stuck in a few sprigs of bamboo for camouflage, as if the VC didn't already know where we were, and took a breather while I surveyed the rice paddy stretching out in front of me toward the mountains, now turned black with the disappearing sun.

A tree line furred the horizon on the far side of the rice field. A second tree line to the north angled off ninety degrees from the first in an L and, farther up, abutted the tree line in which Mike Company had established its defenses, forming a kind of U around the rice. The tree lines were black ink sketches in the gathering dusk.

I added a few touches to my hole by fashioning a little shelf in the side for my grenades and extra ammo magazines, then moved into my new home by the uncomplicated process of sitting in it with my M-14 propped up where I could reach it.

Sergeant Shireman came by, checking the line. "Split-level, two-car garage," he quipped, moving on.

Vietnam started changing colors with the fall of night. I always liked to watch it. The brilliant green of rice paddies and bamboo and jungle patches faded as the sun merged gradually with the monsoon-season skud of dirty black clouds on the horizon. Stabbing rays of sunshine, muted and weak now, shot wildly across the sky until, bruised by the clouds, they turned scarlet and then violet. The land itself then turned bruised-looking through a dark purple haze. After that, quickly, the blackness came and there was no more color.

The black time was the danger time. Victor Charlie came out of his holes and started sniffing around.

> You gotta get yourself a weapon,
> An automatic weapon . . .
> 'Cause every night when you're sleepin',
> Charlie Cong comes a-creepin'
> . . . all around.

It was during the time of the dark purple haze, while I was sitting in my new hole with my mind ten thousand miles away to where a girl actually *wore* the perfume I kept stored in an extra shirt in my packboard, that a disembodied voice yelling in Vietnamese from somewhere in the rice paddy jerked me abruptly back to the war. Reaching for Matilda, I sat up straight and peered into the haze. I couldn't see anything, of course, except the outline of the mountains and the darker ink of the tree lines.

I hadn't thought anything short of mortar rounds exploding underneath them could have stirred my Ruff Puffs from their hammocks. I was wrong. One of them suddenly jumped up, grabbed his Thompson submachine gun, and stomped out of the bamboo toward the shrilling voice in the rice paddy. Apparently a sensitive little guy offended by something the VC said, he started windmilling his arms angrily and shouting back at the voice, indignant but not *too* indignant. He didn't want to do anything as foolish as charging into the rice in pursuit of the Viet Cong orator.

Frenchy was amused. "Must have called him a water buffalo fucker or something," he quipped from his hole.

The furious war of epithets raged between the stiff-spined little Ruff Puff and the unseen Vietnamese in the rice paddy. Amazed by the exchange, Marines on the line sat up and listened, wondering. When the PF could no longer bear the insults, he whipped up his submachine gun sideways to counter muzzle climb and ripped off several staccato bursts from the hip.

To everyone's even more considerable surprise, the Viet Cong in the rice popped up like a gopher from its hole and replied with a burst of his own at the Ruff Puff. Then, before anyone could react, the VC pivoted and fired toward the tree line at the end of the U on Mike Company's right flank.

What the hell was he doing?

The VC vanished into the rice like a mouse into its hole after stealing the cheese just as Marines opened up in his direction with a thundering crescendo of rifle and automatic weapons fire. Tracers slashed through the rice like scythes.

There was blistering fire in return. It came from the tree line at the end of the U. In the gathering darkness, muzzle flashes blossomed like radiant jungle flowers.

We were in for some deep shit. From the sound of the firing, there must be an entire fucking regiment of NVA out there!

Mike Company hurled everything it had at the tree line. The tree line hurled everything it had back at us. The clash and thunder of all-out combat numbed the senses. Machine gun fire boiled the ground around our holes. Singing lead started harvesting the bamboo. It came toppling down.

The hole I had dug was not much larger than a bread box. Nonetheless, the two PFs somehow found space at the bottom of it to curl up like fetuses unwilling to be ejected from the womb.

I just knew human waves were preparing to come charging across the paddies.

It hadn't dawned on me right away, but there was something wrong. Tracers crisscrossing the field, like some kind of light show, were all *red,* coming and going.

The enemy used *green* tracers.

I knew what was wrong when I heard an ONTOS engine cranking up in the opposing tree line. A fifty-caliber spotter round hurled by and crashed through the trees behind us. The next sound we heard would be that of a 106 exploding on our asses.

The bad guys didn't have ONTOS.

I thought of the friendly fire at Cam Ne.

We were fighting other Marines. *That* was what the VC planned when he fired at both tree lines—deceiving us into fighting each other.

Realization had also dawned on the sergeants. They scurried along the line like frantic ants shouting and fanning their arms. Sergeant Shireman leaped from one hole to another, grabbing men and shaking them until they let up on the trigger.

*"Goddamnit, cease fire! You shitbirds! You dumb fucks! Stop your fucking shooting. Cease fire! That's Lima Company over there."*

What a fucked-up war.

"Jee-suz Kee-rist!" I heard as the shooting tapered off and plunged into dead silence.

Somewhere out there in the darkness of Viet Cong time a little VC private must have been laughing his ass off at what he had done.

It was the biggest firefight I had seen in Vietnam.

My heart was thundering in my chest and I felt something sharpening its claws in my belly. Breathing deeply to keep from hyperventilating, I leaned back in my hole on top of the Ruff Puffs. One of them stuck his head up, tentatively, to make sure it was all over. That was when I thought I must be hallucinating.

I smelled Rita. It was such a powerful sensation that I caught myself looking around to see if she were really there. All I saw was the cowering Ruff Puffs.

My eyes fell on my pack lying to one side of the hole. Then I understood. Machine gun fire had stitched the pack; friendly fire was giving it a beating. I opened the flap with a sinking feeling of loss and found Rita's perfume shattered.

For the next few weeks, everywhere I went I smelled like a New Orleans whorehouse.

"Oh, Roberts! You don't know what you *do* to me," O'Brien the Arab gushed every time he got near.

# Chapter 11

My LITTLE PIECE of the Crotch, the by-God U.S. Fightin'
Marines, did not talk much anymore about kicking VC ass.
The platoon was operating at about two-thirds strength, what
with the casualties we had been suffering one or two at a
time for the past few months. Instead of kicking ass, we
were more occupied with saving ass. Our own.

One patrol merged into another in a murky stream of time
muddied and clotted by fatigue, sickness, and a gnawing fear
that accompanied us like death's heads into the nighttime
VC jungles and rice paddies. I had been shitting rice water
for a month. A chance glance now and then into some still
pool of water reflected the image of a gaunt blond stranger
who was nineteen years old but looked an ancient thirty.

I thought it had just been O'Brien and Frenchy and Bruce
and the others who looked that way.

The luminous dial of my watch told me it was a few
minutes before midnight. On another of its endless patrols,

the platoon forded a jungle stream and crept along a trail flanked on one side by thick jungle and on the other by a cane field. The sugar cane was about eight feet tall. A full moon had been shining down on us in between playing hide-and-seek with scudding monsoon clouds. The clouds were winning. The moon disappeared and a steady drizzle began. It rained every night now, and most days. It seemed we could never get dry. That only added to our misery.

The patrol halted. Word came down the file using hand-and-arm signals, almost the only form of communication used in the bush, that there was an antipersonnel mine on the gate ahead. We had become adept at spotting them. The engineer team made its way forward to the gate, past the Marines who, instead of getting down and setting up security, leaned on their rifles with weary heads dropped chin against chest. Two or three cupped their hands and attempted to light soggy C-ration cigarettes. Their faces reflected the stark glow of the matches.

The platoon had grown careless in the way that marked tired warriors who had been here long enough to water down terror to nothing but a curious little fear that curled up sometimes and slept fitfully just below your stomach, like some furry creature in its burrow. It could wake in an instant and churn hell out of your guts, but the rest of the time it slept and only stretched out its sharp claws now and then to let you know it was still in its lair.

I kept nursing a sixth sense feeling that we were not alone in the Viet Cong night, but I neither saw nor heard anything to trigger alarm no matter how intently I listened and peered into the dense jungle on the right or the cane field on the left. Jittery, I stepped cautiously off the trail into the deeper shadows of the jungle growth. Rain pattered on plants.

At that instant the night split apart.

Gunfire exploded from the cane. My little furry creature in the gut awoke with sharp claws all extended, like a scared cat attached to a screen door.

*"Ambush left! Ambush left!!"* It was either Sergeant

Shireman or squad leader Corporal Bellot, shouting instructions.

The standard immediate action drill for a near ambush like this was to assault into it, every gun blazing. If you hit the ground, the enemy mopped you up where you lay. If you ran, the blocking force got you. In this instance, the impenetrable jungle was the blocking force. That meant, illogical as it seemed, that you charged directly into the teeth of death. There was no other choice. We had been through practice drills so many times in training that it was second nature.

*"Go! Go! Go!"* yelled the voice in the night.

We obeyed.

Yelling and screaming to pump up the adrenaline to do what no sane, logical man would ever do.

I crashed through the wet cane like a madman, shrieking and pumping shots on automatic in front of me as I went. Squeezing the trigger, waltzing Matilda, at shadows that flitted, that skulked, that flew, that sent back death.

I screamed at the terrible shadows. I sprayed them with lead.

Running.

Running straight into the enemy's muzzle flashes.

Running at ghosts who bled but then vanished before your eyes after you shot them.

I hardly felt the blast of sharp pain that shot through the nerves of my lower right calf. I stumbled, almost went down, but kept going. If you fell behind, the gooks came like bogey men and strung you up in a tree and stuffed your balls in your mouth.

I reached the other side of the cane field. I was hobbling. I had stopped yelling. The gooks were gone, melting as always into the night that was their friend and our enemy. The rest of the platoon emerged from the cane in ragged, unnerved bunches, coming out and standing at a dike that rose and then fell into a flooded rice paddy. I heard them panting and wheezing like winded horses. Some of them sent futile shots across the paddy.

I became aware of pain in my leg. It felt like every nerve ending had been exposed.

"Doc?" I called in a loud whisper.

It wasn't necessary to whisper now, but whispering had become second nature in the bush, like hand-and-arm signals.

Doc Lindstrom had night blindness. I heard him floundering in the cane, the last man through it. Blind as he was, night patrols must have been a special kind of hell for him.

"Doc?" That was to guide him. He bumped into me before he realized where I was.

"That you, Roberts? You hit?"

"I must have been." I thought a bullet would feel different. "It's my leg, Doc. Can you check it out?"

The leg was getting numb. I moaned slightly, almost afraid to look.

"Doc?"

"Be still, Roberts."

The eerie glow from his red lens played on my leg. I didn't see any blood. I held his light for him while he cut the trouser leg away and rolled it up over a sliver of rotted bamboo protruding awkwardly from the flesh on the inside of my leg.

"Punji stake," Doc said, looking up from the red glow of light. "It hit the bone."

In the background I heard Sergeant Shireman and Lieutenant Rowe reorganizing and getting out security while they did a head count and checked on casualties. Incredibly enough, I was the only wounded. Our discovery of the mine on the gate, instead of tripping it off, and the moon hiding behind the clouds, had apparently disorganized the ambush.

There were no VC casualties lying around either.

"Doc, does this mean I get Medevac'd?" I asked.

"Naw. I'll pull it out and put on a battle dressing. Check with me in the morning when we get back to Giang Dong."

The next morning when Doc took off the dressing to

check, the wound was an angry, seeping red hole. He opened it wide with his finger and filled it with bacitracin antibiotic ointment.

"It'll get worse before it gets better," he predicted.

That proved to be an understatement. We didn't know much about punji stakes then.

# Chapter 12

I DREW AN ASSIGNMENT to escort five ARVN soldiers to Mieu Dong, a checkpoint on Highway One about four miles south of the Phong Le Bridge, where I would link up to fight with a Combined Action Company until relieved. It was not a choice assignment. The ARVN had a reputation. They would *di-di mao* on you when the shit came down and leave you to do the flushing.

"You won't have any Americans with you for a while," the company liaison officer advised me during his briefing. "They're a raggedy-ass bunch, but do what you can. Check in on the radio with battalion net three times a day and twice at night."

I started out of the tent, feeling less than elated.

"Uh, Corporal Roberts?" By this time I had been promoted to lance corporal.

"Yes, sir."

"Good luck."

"Am I gonna need it, sir?"

"Maybe."

George Renninger had also drawn a CAC assignment. I learned later he fell right into his role and was actually made mayor of a Vietnamese village.

My five ARVNs stood around smoking smelly Vietnamese cigarettes outside the company CP tent. They were clad in tight-legged, tiger-striped fatigues and armed with a curious combination of WWII weapons—a Browning light 30-caliber machine gun, a Browning Automatic Rifle, an M-1 Garand, and an M-1 carbine. The fifth trooper carried the 30-cal tripod and support gear.

The Vietnamese were small; not one of the troopers weighed much more than a hundred pounds. By this time, I didn't weigh a whole lot more either, although considerably taller, and I loaded myself down with twice as much gear as they were humping before we started out. I had bandoleers of ammo strung over my shoulders, a case of C-rats strapped to my packboard, all the frag grenades I could carry, and my Kipling stuck deep into my pack. I thought this might be an adventure Kipling would appreciate.

The ARVN interpretor at company ordered the tiger stripes to follow me, then, with a shrug, wished me luck with them and stayed behind. We started out of Giang Dong beneath a cloudy sky with me on point. Limping a little from the punji wound, I shot an azimuth and pursued the compass needle across a paddy and along a wide dike.

We were filing across a small cemetery of big bowl-like graves when I heard what sounded like sobbing. I stopped and looked back. The Vietnamese with the 30-cal machine gun was falling behind with his burden. He looked about to cry.

The machine gun *was* heavy for such a small fellow. I took it and handed him my lighter M-14. He seemed grateful.

We had not proceeded much further before I heard more sobbing. This time it was the soldier with the BAR. Annoyed, I nonetheless relieved him of the weapon. "Gimme that!" Now I was carrying the 30-cal *and* the BAR.

It would be dark within an hour. I picked up the pace to avoid being caught in the VC night with *these* troops. That brought on whining and complaints from the ARVN with the M-1 Garand. The more I tried to ignore him, the more vocal he became. What did they think I was—their pack mule? Smitty might have carried everything for them with a grin. I wouldn't.

I finally halted in my tracks, sweating beneath my own double burden. My leg felt like someone was jabbing it with a bayonet. Growing more angry by the second, I finally gave up trying to control my temper and turned on my charges. They huddled together like village chickens. They might not have understood the words, but they had little difficulty comprehending the content. I finished by throwing their weapons on the ground, grabbing my M-14 back, onto which I calmly fixed a bayonet. The ARVN cast apprehensive glances at each other as I stalked to the back of the file, bayonet gleaming.

*"Di di mao . . . di di now!"* I shouted, jabbing at the shirkers.

After that, I started wondering if I could keep up with *them*.

There was a checkpoint in a rusty tin building on the outskirts of Mieu Dong; we reached it just before the sun left and the night started to change the colors of the sky. A short distance beyond the tin building rose the rough stone walls of a courtyard nestled among a scattering of palms painted against a brilliant Oriental sunset. The only part of the Buddhist temple visible behind the walls was its elaborate roof on top of which carved dragons were mounted.

An ARVN Ranger with yellow sergeant stripes pinned to his pocket flap stepped briskly from the shadows of the temple and stopped us at the courtyard gate.

*"Dong lai."*

The sergeant was small like all Vietnamese, only considerably more muscular, with a face as fierce-looking as those of the carved dragons. He carefully scrutinized identification from the Vietnamese replacements before he barked a command that sent them double-timing into the temple compound. Then he turned his fierce face on me.

"You Marine," he observed in passable English with a French accent that reminded me of Frenchy Michaud. I was already homesick.

No shit.

"I Nguyen Hai," he introduced himself, adding, "Numbah one *sar-jon*."

I introduced myself. Asians shake limp-wristed. Nguyen Hai was no exception.

"Ro-bear," he repeated.

"Is your tee wee here?"

The lieutenant was. *"Oui.* You come."

The wall surrounding the temple and a square stone tower about two stories tall was topped with broken glass imbedded in concrete. Sandbagged in on the flat top of the tower, a 50-caliber machine gun thrust its long black snout out from the perimeter of the village that surrounded the fortification. The gunner lay on sandbags, obviously asleep.

Near the tower in the center of the compound squatted a single 105mm howitzer with five rounds of corroded ammo staked next to it for all to see. I had encountered this strange phenomenon before. The ammo would never be used. It seemed cannon ammunition had become something of a status symbol. Like money. The more you had, the more status you held.

The "sar-jon" led the way into the temple. It was one room dimly lighted containing a table on top of which were two military radios, a field phone, a map, and a transistor radio. Vietnamese music warbled from the transistor radio.

The tee wee in green fatigues and shower shoes did not bother to get out of his hammock strung across the back of the room.

Nguyen made introductions. "Tee Wee Van," he said. "He numbah one *officier*." But the sergeant stood behind the tee wee's back when he said that. The tee wee did not see him wink at me.

Nguyen translated the officer's response: "He say welcome to Mieu Dong camp. He also say you go on patrol tomorrow and he stay here to hear radios."

It figured.

The sergeant tried to be helpful in getting me settled in, but all it took was my spreading a poncho on the floor among the ARVNs' straw mats. Nguyen left to return shortly with some candles and a guitar. The candles lent a warm glow to the faces of the dozen or so Vietnamese soldiers who gathered around, squatting on their haunches, as the sergeant began plucking on the guitar with stubbed fingers.

"Hai know numbah one American song," he promised. "You see."

The Rangers in the candlelight smiled and clapped their hands in childish delight. Nguyen began singing without further formalities:

> Oh, my da-ling, oh, my da-ling,
> Oh, my da-ling Cremintine,
> Vous are los' an' gone fo-evah,
> Oh, my da-ling Cremintine!

The audience applauded and giggled like a covey of Girl Scouts. After a few more songs, the Rangers passed around a bottle of Tiger Piss and some *Bai Muoi Bai* beer. The Tiger Piss burned all the way down. Then Nguyen ran his troops off to their mats with an admonishment.

"Sleep now," he said. "Tomorrow, maybe we kill beau-coup VC."

He grinned. The Rangers grinned, but not nearly with the same enthusiasm.

I remember wondering if the VC ever struck Mieu Dong camp. I also wondered how many defenders in the compound were on watch.

Thank God I didn't know the answer to these questions before I drifted off to sleep.

# Chapter 13

THAT THE VIETNAMESE RANGERS, Biet Dong Quons, or BDQs as they were known to the Marines, the elite of the Army of the Republic of Vietnam, were a raggedy-ass bunch at best, cast no favorable light on the rest of the army. The trust I had initially in Sergeant Nguyen Hai was to deepen into friendship while the feelings of trepidation I held for his troops were to remain unchanged.

"You speak good English," I noted of the little fierce man the next morning while his Rangers prepared for our first mission together.

Our mission, translated through Nguyen from the tee wee, was to escort a government tax collector around to the hamlets in the district to collect rice tax imposed on farmers. The tax collector had not yet arrived.

"*Oui*. I speak English, French, and many Vietnamese," Nguyen replied. "I learn English from Americans in Saigon long time past."

We were standing together in the cool morning in front of the temple, our packs and weapons on the ground nearby, ready to go. Nguyen lit a cigarette and idly observed the smoke that trailed up from where he held the cigarette pinched between thumb and finger. The smoke transported him back in time.

"What about French?" I asked.

There was a scar at the edge of his lips that crinkled whenever he smiled. It crinkled now, but only briefly.

"I with French paratroopers fighting Viet Minh," he explained. "Hai at Dien Bien Phu," he added, watching me from the corners of his eyes to catch my reaction.

Every Marine in Vietnam by now knew the story of how communist forces on the "Plain of Jars" surrounded the French in a battle that was decisive in driving them from Vietnam. Most of the defenders either died in the battle or were executed after they surrendered. Even mentioning the name Dien Bien Phu was sufficient to bring sober looks to a new generation of foreigners fighting on the peninsula.

"Did you get captured?" I asked Nguyen.

"Hai escape before last day. Hai go Hanoi."

As though it were no more difficult than catching a bus. After the downfall of the French, many of the Vietnamese who had fought the communists filtered north to merge into the population and escape retributions. Most had since returned to again fight commies. I looked upon the little soldier with new regard.

The tax collector wore horm-rimmed glasses, a white shirt, black slacks, and carried a briefcase and a haughty expression on his face. I thought his head preposterously large for the rest of his body. He spoke a few words to the tee wee, but ignored everyone else, standing aside impatiently while the patrol organized. Government service anywhere in the world seemed to breed arrogance and disrespect.

I immediately disliked and distrusted the man.

Some Ruff Puffs from the local Popular Forces accompanied the patrol to be dropped off at the first village. They refused to travel the roads unescorted. Sometimes, when Marines took fire from a "friendly" village, we were not sure whether it came from VC who ran and hid or VC disguised as Popular Defense Forces.

It was a stroll on a sunny day. The ARVNs bore their weapons casually over their shoulders or at sling arms and chattered gaily among themselves as we walked the surly tax man from hamlet to hamlet. None of the villagers appeared to like the collector very much. He talked briefly, business-like, to the village chief of each hamlet, opened his briefcase and exchanged a receipt for piastres, then closed his brief-case and indicated he was ready to continue. It was an effective, direct method of taxation.

Late in the afternoon as we approached the last ville of the day and the monsoon clouds were gathering on the horizon, I detected a marked change in the patrol. The chatter ceased suddenly and the Rangers unslung their arms. Whereas the column earlier resembled a class of school children on a nature hike, it now spread out into a combat formation. Only the tax man appeared unconcerned. He strode silently along pumping his short arms and keeping to himself as he had all day.

I asked Nguyen what was happening.

"We not come this village before this day," he said. "Maybe VC in village. We see soon."

I felt the little furry creature in my gut start to stir.

The patrol came to a curve in the road that swept toward a peaceful-appearing clump of thatch-roofed hootches be-yond a closed bamboo gate. Nguyen called a halt while he walked a little ways up the road and studied the settlement. The tax collector frowned and started pacing back and forward, glancing at his watch, the perfect picture of an executive who did not have time for this kind of nonsense.

Finally, shoulders squared, chin jutted, he stomped up to Nguyen. The two Vietnamese argued and gesticulated at the village. It ended with the government man angrily marching toward the ville, like someone fleeing a lover's spat. A shadow fell across the sun.

"He say, no VC there," Nguyen interpreted. "Hai say maybe beaucoup VC, but he say, follow."

There were seven Rangers in the patrol, all tense and alert as we entered through the gate. Rifle safeties clicked to "fire," although everything remained unthreatening. Water buffalo wandered on the outskirts and skinny chickens scratched in the dirt. The huts closed around us, then opened in a big circle at the center. The Rangers' eyes kept darting. The tax man's were glued unwaveringly ahead.

I could not help feeling we were walking into a trap. I dismissed the feeling momentarily by attributing it to the spooky way the ARVN were behaving.

The feeling returned stronger than ever when three stone-faced Vietnamese men dressed in city civvies met us beneath the trees in the town square. Elders with gray chin whiskers had met us everywhere else. These men were of an age to be either South Vietnamese Army or Viet Cong. They did not look like ARVN. Their contemplative dark eyes swept the patrol one by one, lingering over the American. I felt hair standing to attention on my arms. My little furry creature kneaded his claws. Casually, as though by accident, I let my M-14 come to bear on the men to let them know they died first if anything went down. Then I thought about it and let Matilda drift slightly until the muzzle centered on the tax man.

I was betting on his being undercover VC—and a ranking one at that. Nervy little bastard. Probably collecting for the South Vietnamese and the VC at the same time.

"Hai," I whispered, "if they ain't VC, there ain't no VC in Vietnam."

We were closed in. Nguyen lighted a cigarette. His hand shook.

"Say nothing," he advised from the corner of his mouth. "We go soon."

I glimpsed several other men standing in doorways and behind huts. My finger was on the trigger. We knew who they were and they knew we knew who they were. Our only advantage was that we had their leaders in our sights. That made it a standoff. Apparently, discretion called for everyone to pretend that nothing was wrong.

Under the circumstances, that was all right with me.

The next few minutes passed like hours.

The tax collector was more jolly than I had seen him all day. I don't think he was pretending. He gave the three men some papers, but the men did not return money as other village leaders had. Within a few minutes, business completed and no questions asked, we started out of the village on the heels of the tax collector. I kept my rifle on him. The small of my back itched where I half expected the first AK round to strike.

I did not breath easily again until we were back at the Buddhist temple.

"Hai, he VC," I said. "What you do?"

"Nothing now," the sergeant said, but a crafty glint entered his eye. "Hai see soon."

I left it at that. This, here, was the ARVNs' war; I was just here to work with them and keep a link between the two armies. But I wasn't alone in giving a sigh of relief when the tax man, with a last word to the tee wee and a scalding look at me, gathered his black briefcase underneath his arm and left. I little realized that we would be meeting again, under circumstances considerably more in my favor.

After dark, a company of Marines on perimeter around some village called for a fire mission to illuminate the night sky with 81mm and 105mm parachute flares. The bright little suns slowly descended on the distant horizon, leaving ragged smoke contrails inscribed in their wake.

It was a good war where I was because all remained quiet at Mieu Dong. The Vietnamese were snoring on their straw mats, the gunner on the 50-cal was sleeping on his sandbags, and the tee wee stretched in his hammock. Only Sergeant Nguyen Hai remained awake; finally he, too, came in and went to bed.

I listened to Nancy Sinatra's voice on my transistor radio, taking me back home:

. . . These boots are made for walkin' . . .

# Chapter 14

GRENADES WERE MY FAVORITE WEAPON. The enemy could not tell where they came from, and they packed a hell of a wallop.

In the night, my patrol of ARVN Rangers came off Highway One and pushed through the rice paddies and jungle until we came to a tree line near a village sympathetic to the VC. The trail leaving the village made a good ambush site. We set up in the bamboo next to the trail. I would initiate the ambush with a grenade while the BAR fired the length of the trail and the riflemen did mop-up. Nguyen and two Rangers set up a blocking force by hiding in a cemetery about fifty meters away in the direction we figured any survivors might try to escape. Unlike Marines, who were trained to assault into a near ambush, the VC returned a small amount of fire and faded away if they could.

Lying flat on my stomach, I waited in the darkness, relieved that it was not raining.

And I waited.

A good soldier did not think about the scent of perfume or

of how it felt to hold a girl in his arms—or of how it felt not to be afraid.

Or of going home.

A good soldier tried not to think when he was waiting for the enemy to come in the night, the only link between other human beings and himself a long commo wire. When I spotted the enemy I would tug on the wire to make sure the other ambushers were awake and ready.

I was dog-tired, as always, my bowels growled and rumbled so loudly from dysentery and parasites that I thought surely any potential victim must hear and avoid us, and my leg throbbed.

Lying weary and sick on my belly in the heat of that VC night, I let a thought slip through that had been playing around in my brain for a long time seeking acknowledgment. I'd kept pushing it away before. But now it appeared for the first time, in bold print inscribed across the inside of the front of my skull: I AIN'T GETTING OUT ALIVE!

*I am getting out alive.*

I AIN'T GETTING OUT ALIVE!

It startled me, appearing like that. I had to catch my breath to control it. I glanced anxiously about, trying to find something familiar to latch onto. There was nothing except the night and the village and the usual bamboo gate—all too familiar but still strange and threatening. I could not even see the man next to me in the ambush line. I would have liked to touch him, just for the contact, but instead I fingered the hard wool and steel of the Thompson submachine gun Nguyen had lent me, and the thin slick strand of wire that connected all of us, like multiple births on an umbilical cord.

Three hours passed. It was after two A.M. when two shadows separated from the village and paused at the bamboo gate. They were armed. In the darkness, I saw rifle protrusions from the black-clad figures. They moved some and I thought one of them carried the SKS carbine manufactured in China or Russia.

I tugged on the commo wire. There should have been an answering tug, but the wire remained slack. I eased the pin from my grenade and held the spoon in place while I waited for the two VC to decide what they were going to do.

I hoped the Rangers were awake and had simply neglected to signal back.

I tugged the wire again. It slithered loose, giving more slack.

The VC unlatched the bamboo gate and started down the trail. They entered the kill zone. It was now or never.

The spoon *pinged* when I lobbed the grenade behind the walking figures and buried my head in my arms to protect my eyes from the flash. The grenade thudded on earth. One of the VC cried out an instant before the grenade exploded.

The explosion should have triggered a deadly burst of BAR and rifle fire from the Rangers. Instead, the silent darkness closed back in immediately.

I realized I was alone. Grabbing the Thompson, I emptied a magazine in rapid bursts to spray the trail where the enemy should have gone down. The dancing muzzle flashes blinded me.

I listened while I quickly changed magazines. Groaning and dragging sounds. Incredible. You shot them, but they never stayed shot.

I fired some more, than heard Nguyen Hai and his two men open up from the cemetery. There was silence afterward—just a dog barking in the village. The inhabitants themselves knew enough to stay inside whenever the shooting started. It was time to get the hell out. I ran down the tree line. The Rangers were gone; I hadn't even heard them pack up and leave.

Like slipping out on an unpaid bill.

*They'd pay,* I promised, seething with rage as I exited the bamboo tree line to the rear and found my way to our rally point on the flat top of a low dike. I did not have to wait long before Nguyen and his blocking force crashed out of the bush. They were panting. I hid until I was certain of them, then stood up. Nguyen carried his own rifle and an SKS thrown over his other shoulder. I was too furious to be interested in an obvious enemy body count.

"Where the hell are they, Hai?" I demanded in a screaming whisper. "I was the only one there during the ambush."

The fierce little sergeant hesitated. "Hai not know," he said. "They maybe same-same VC."

"I'll kill them!" I vowed.

"No. Hai kill them."

It was not the time nor place for a discussion. Other VC in the area would be looking for us. And now we were only four.

Moving out, I led the way quickly down the dike until we came to the highway, which we paralleled in the tree line back to Mieu Dong. The VC liked to ambush the ambushers when they were returning to base, but I was too angry and tired to give a damn. Every muscle in my body—muscles I did not know I had—ached from the stress of too many days and nights in the bush.

The sun was up and shining on the temple dragons when we reached the compound. Sergeant Nguyen had seemingly remained indifferent about our missing ambush patrol until we found the Rangers asleep on their grass mats. He turned into a raving lunatic. Hurling his wiry body at the malefactors, he delivered a flurry of kicks and punches that sent the ARVN soldiers scrambling in retreat and soon left them bloody and contrite and huddled like chickens against the outer temple where he held them at the point of the bayonet on the captured SKS. I knew by the looks on their faces that he was threatening to execute them.

I was too beat to care anymore. I stumbled into the temple. Tee Wee Van lolled drunkenly at the radio table with a bottle of liquor in front of him and a nubile young girl on his lap. He waved and smiled. I spread my poncho in a corner and started clawing at my boot laces.

I didn't even look at him.

Nguyen came inside before I finished getting my boots off.

"They say them come home because they don't like ambush patrol," he explained, looking embarrassed. "They say night patrol bad."

I glanced up and shrugged. "Night is when the VC are out."

"Hai know that," he said. "Tomorrow, them know that, too, *mon ami*. Tomorrow Hai train soldiers."

He held up a tightly clenched fist.

"Next patrol them be numbah one. They not be afraid of VC. They be afraid of *Hai*."

I rolled up in my poncho. The last thing I heard was the girl giggling on Tee Wee Van's lap.

# Chapter 15

IT WAS AN EERIE kind of war. There were many names like "The Valley of the Shadow of Death" to describe places of particular awe or fascination. A lieutenant and a sergeant from regiment arrived at Mieu Dong camp one morning to brief me on a new mission to a particularly forbidding place north of Da Nang.

My mission was to recon the area around what appeared on the map to be a man-made installation—a factory or a refinery—located in isolation near the coast on the Hai Van Peninsula. The lieutenant's thick finger stubbed at a valley on the old French map he had brought along. In the early days of the war, French maps were often all that was available.

"Your patrol will be inserted here by H-34 helicopter tomorrow at 0700," the lieutenant said. "Extraction will be at your request, or you can walk out along the beach to Da Nang. We want you to update the map and sketch this installation, whatever it is."

"That's VC country," I realized. "That's . . ."

The sergeant grinned wryly and spoke for almost the first time. "Yes," he said. "That's the Valley of the Shadow of Death."

I grinned back to show the name did not affect me. "Verily, though I walk through the valley of the shadow of death, I shall fear no evil . . ."

". . . 'Cause you're the meanest sonofabitch in the valley."

"You got it."

The BDQs did not feel that way. They made it obvious the next morning when they fell in for pre-mission inspection that they did not want to go. They made an absurd army. Some wore tiger stripes and tennis shoes. Others had donned green fatigue bottoms with colorful sports shirts. Other uniforms were completed with a curious assortment of shower shoes, berets, cowboy hats, helmets, and a Dodgers baseball cap. They were armed with M-14s, an M-1 with a cleaning rod stuck down the barrel—"Keep dust out"—a Thompson submachine gun with a broken stock, the heavy BAR on a bipod, and one killer had a dozen knives strapped all over his body.

Two men were holding hands. One man was crying. A short man had his pack strapped to a bicycle, and a taller one had two live ducks in a ruck. A third clutched a squawking chicken.

Stunned, I turned to Nguyen Hai.

"They to eat," was the automatic answer. Even Sergeant Nguyen—*he* did not want to go.

"How in hell can we go on patrol sounding like a poultry farm?" I demanded.

"No sweat," Hai said matter-of-factly. "VC alla time know we come anyhow."

I began to sputter, made speechless by the marked contrast between the raggedy-ass bunch before me now and the Marines back in Mike Company—weary and disease-ridden as those Marines might be. I found my voice and began to shout at the patrol, spitting droplets and shaking my fist. The chicken squawked louder.

I paused to catch my breath and let Nguyen translate. The sergeant barked a few words, condensing the English, and then looked toward me to continue.

"You weren't translating word for word," I accused. "What did you tell them?"

"I tell them you will kill them," Nguyen said innocently, adding casually after a pause, "Them believe you."

What the hell. I selected eight of the best men, including Nguyen Hai. The H-34 made three false landings to confuse the enemy before it discharged the nine-man patrol in a clearing on a saddle between two hills. I led the way in a limping run from the LZ and weasled into a wild canebrake to listen for movement and watch our backtrail. I sent out scouts for a quick recon, then, satisfied that the insertion had not been witnessed, I shot a compass azimuth for the opposite side of the valley toward the mysterious installation by the coast.

The terrain was different than the rice paddies, dikes, and bamboo jungle I was accustomed to in the lowlands. It was heavy bush, jungle where vines and lianas grappled with the forest, and bamboo thickets. Hard going, but it wasn't as bad as some of the second growth jungle that grew farther inland.

Wild country. Yet, there appeared to be little wildlife. Almost no birds. No monkeys. If it hadn't been for the burr of insects, there would have been nothing but an awful silence.

The patrol grew jittery. Rangers whispered among themselves and sometimes held hands and tried to cluster on breaks. Their behavior made me uneasy. I remembered how they had *di-di mao'd* on me the night of the ambush. What I would have given for a "few good men" instead of these Vietnamese who tried to take ducks and chickens on patrol and who may or may not fight when the time came.

We cut no enemy sign. I kept away from the few trails that threaded through the low places. Trudging through the growing heat of the day that always preceded the late afternoon rains, we worked our way cautiously across the valley toward the coast some seven kilometers away. Occasionally I glassed the countryside and made corrections to the French map. Unconsciously, I began to hurry, finding myself almost as anxious as the BDQs to rid myself of this place. Something about it was oppressive, threatening. It was like we were being watched by an invisible enemy.

Coming upon the crashed helicopter at the bottom of the hill did not help the mood any. An old B-model Huey, it had been there for a long time. It squatted nose angled up in the trees, its rotor broken and part of it missing. Everything glass had been broken out of it. Vines and other vegetation crept in and around it. Mold and gray moss had caught hold inside past the hollow eyes of the windows where pilots— *American* pilots—had once strapped themselves in to fly over VC land.

It was like finding the place where the elephants all went to die, this place of the old helicopter's graveyard. The only thing lacking was a human skeleton strapped at the controls, grinning its death grin down at us.

Nguyen whispered, "Boss, *mon ami,* the boys them want to go from here."

The BDQs were white-eyeing the forest around us.

"Why are they so afraid of an old helicopter?" I asked.

"This valley is place of dark," Nguyen replied seriously. "That what them say."

"That's what the VC wants them to say," I reasoned.

Nonetheless, I was also eager to have this place behind me.

The patrol moved on through wild country, breaking trail. In the early afternoon, we came to the valley's east wall and began to climb through heavy forest. I could not dislodge the feeling that we were being watched, although we still had seen no enemy sign.

We sweated furiously. The patrol was evenly spaced from point to tail to keep an ambush from catching everyone. The file moved fast, almost at a dog trot. Every man was eager to crest and leave the valley and come to the coast. The fear we felt might be nameless, but it was real nonetheless. The little furry creature in my gut was working its claws.

We almost made it.

Then, the drums began beating. First, one in solo, drumming in slow rhythm, muffled by the forest, not far away. Another joined in, more distant than the first. They beat in counterpoint. Dum DUM dum DUM dum DUM . . . Others hurried to add their voices to the odd jungle symphony. It was the VC warning telegraph.

Raw terror ripped through the patrol. In another instant my Rangers would be scattering like panicked mice. I quickly calculated our chances of survival. To return to the valley was to be trapped in almost certain death. Our only hope lay ahead, up to the crest, out of the valley. The high ground.

Decision made, I sprinted along the patrol, grabbing men by their clothing and jerking them ahead until I got them running. There was no longer need for caution. We had been discovered.

"Hai! Keep them together or we're all dead."

I led the way up, panting beneath my pack. The drumbeats surrounded us—ghostly, eerie, disembodied sounds. They were beating faster, almost frantically, signaling our escape attempt.

I had seen the drums before; once I even slept inside one to get out of the rain. They were enormous hollowed-out logs with holes cut in them here and there to release the sound. I had seen them, but I had never heard them.

I hoped never to hear them again.

I thumbed the safety of my M-14 to OFF. Whistles began to shrill behind us. Shouts. Sporadic rifle fire. I preferred this to the drums.

The drums continued to beat.

The VC were in pursuit, like hounds on a fresh trail.

I was the first man to reach the top of the mountain and discover the hopelessness of our predicament. There was a small semi-clearing at the very crest. Beyond, east, lay the coast. But it may as well have been a thousand miles away.

107

There was another forested valley in between—and the drums were there, too.

From the increasing volume of shouting, whistle blasts, gunfire, and other noises, I estimated my patrol had been trapped by a company-sized VC unit, eighty to one hundred soldiers. Trapped one step away from getting out of the Valley of the Shadow of Death.

I AIN'T GETTING OUT ALIVE!

I didn't have time to dwell on it. All eight of my men had made it to the top. I set up a hasty defense perimeter around the clearing. The ARVN Rangers, looking petrified, sprawled behind whatever cover they could find and prepared for battle. Like it or not, we had to fight; we could not run in any direction.

The only possible escape, I decided, was by air. I tried to radio for an extraction, but the PRC-10 would not work. Nothing issued from the radio except static. Casting it aside, I found the ARVN RTO on perimeter. He finally got through to his CP on his radio. Relaying a message to Marine HHQ was a complicated and time-consuming matter. Time was running out.

I AIN'T GETTING . . .

*I am!*

I gave Sergeant Nguyen the message in English. Nguyen translated to his RTO, who relayed the message in Vietnamese to BDQ headquarters. BDQ headquarters was then supposed to see that the Marines received my request for immediate helicopter rescue.

After directing the BAR to cover the most likely avenue of enemy approach, I quickly gathered what explosives we had brought—C-4 and twenty pounds of TNT in an engineer's satchel. While the hilltop we were on was partially clear, there was still a lot of small stuff and three or four big trees in the middle. I would have to clear a chopper LZ—and fast!

I grabbed Nguyen. "They've got to hold," I cried, "or we've all bought it."

"Where chopper land?" Nguyen wanted to know.

I jabbed a finger at my feet. "Right here."

"You have plan?"

"Let's hope it works."

I could not be certain our radio message got through, but I had no choice but to operate on the assumption that it had. Working feverishly, I packed explosives low around the trunks of the large trees in the partial clearing, intending to rapidly clear an LZ for the rescue chopper. I linked the charges with detonating cord. While I worked I became aware that the drums had ceased. The VC did not need the drums anymore. The prey was in the trap.

The jungle fell oddly silent while the Viet Cong established positions. By now I knew how the little black-clad men worked. There would be probes to test our strength and will, followed by an assault wave. If the VC felt confident their trap would hold, the assault would not come until after nightfall. Night always belonged to the guerrillas.

After I finished charging the trees, I packed a claymore mine inside the satchel with the remaining explosives and ran down the trail with it. I hid the satchel in bushes and set the claymore for hand clacker detonation. I took the clacker back with me, running out the wire, and prepared it for when I would need it against the attack.

I checked our defense perimeter before setting off the tree explosives. Nguyen had formed the nervous Vietnamese into a formidable defense. Once the trees went down and the VC realized the reason, they would probably throw all caution to the wind and launch an immediate attack. I wasn't sure if the Rangers could hold or not. I kept thinking of the ambush and of the two ducks and a chicken.

For weapons, the patrol had the BAR with several clips of ammo, an M-79 grenade launcher, a few frags per man, and their personal weapons. I carried my M-14.

Several flashes of bright light and a clap of sound sent the big trees in the clearing toppling to the ground. The chopper would not be able to touch down, but it could hover low enough to allow the patrol to scramble into its womb.

If the chopper came.

The instant the trees blew, the VC opened up with small arms fire, a crackle of it, like the magnified sounds of a forest fire. It came from the thick bush all around. Bullets whined and ricocheted. Tracers inscribed quick green marks around us.

How long would it take for them to bring up mortars?

Sergeant Nguyen and I directed the defense, scurrying from man to man. I thought Sergeant Shireman would have been pleased with my performance.

"Conserve ammo. Make it count. Wait for the attack," I said.

The battle was joined. The little force on the hill hurled frags at sounds and squeezed off rounds at flitting shadows. The grenadier popped M-79 grenades into the bush often enough to make the VC wary. The explosions were muffled and invisible in the forest. Even in the daylight, it was the same old thing of fighting ghosts. You never knew if you made a hit. You fired and took fire and the battle continued in the heat of the day.

I was sweating, as always. The Vietnamese tiger stripes I wore were dark with wetness at the armpits and down the back where my pack rested. I crouched behind a log, squinting at the forest, cracking off shots whenever I detected movement.

Shadows. It seemed I had fought the entire war against shadows.

How long before the VC stopped probing and charged? How long could nine men withstand a full company? Had my radio message gotten through?

Remembering the wiremen, I was determined not to be taken alive. I selected my fighting position so I could give a good accounting of myself when and if the time came.

I had to accept the fact that my time might be coming soon, my number might be coming up.

The firefight raged. There were no human sounds now, just the rattle of firearms spiced by the periodic *whump!* of a grenade exploding. I huddled over the ARVN radio attempting to pick up an artillery battery. Failing that, I switched to the frequency used by Marine helicopters.

"Helicopter, this is Black Box Two-Niner . . . Black Box Two-Niner. Can you read, over?"

No reply.

The battle shifted to my side of the perimeter. I scrambled forward to get a better estimate of the situation. Peeking over my log, I glimpsed the trail we used to reach the hilltop. Two VC darted across the trail and into the bushes almost on top of where I'd hidden the satchel charge with the claymore.

I hit the clacker. The enemy soldiers vanished in a terrific explosion of dirt, rock, smoke, and body parts. Pink mist. Debris rained out of the sky for a full ten seconds afterward.

Enemy fire slacked off, but soon picked up again. Our Browning Automatic Rifle chewed up leaves and trees and rocks in short, angry bursts. The VC were closing in for the kill. We fought desperately against the shadows, against the odds, realizing it was hopeless. Clearly, time was on the enemy's side.

A Ranger suffered a superficial leg wound. Automatic rifle fire stitched the log behind which I crouched. A pack lying in the open was repeatedly killed because the VC thought it was a man.

We were not going to return from The Valley of The Shadow of Death. It had been appropriately named.

I AIN'T GETTING . . .

I was the first to hear the chopper. I rolled over on my back to search the skies. Then the BDQs heard it. Their firing slacked off.

"Keep fighting!" I shouted, afraid the ARVN would panic and herd up in the clearing to be slaughtered like goats.

"Keep fighting. Keep your positions."

Nguyen was translating, scrambling around and across the clearing, waving his rifle, threatening to shoot the first man who disobeyed orders. Enemy fire ripped at trees and bush all around him.

It must have reminded him of Dien Bien Phu.

111

I grabbed the radio and dashed to the center of the makeshift LZ.

"Helicopter, this is Black Box Two-Niner . . ."

This time there was an answer: *"Black Box Two-Niner, we saw an explosion. Was that you?"*

"I just set it off. We're on the hilltop. Can you see me?"

The chopper winged into view. High, circling, out of small arms range. I waved my arms to attract its attention while the VC zeroed in on me with automatic fire.

*"Is it a hot LZ?"* the chopper wanted to know.

"It's pretty damned warm."

A pause. *"Black Box, be ready. We're coming in fast."*

The H-34 dropped out of sight behind a hill.

Nguyen and I prepared the men for extraction. They shouldered their rucks and began firing furiously to keep the Viet Cong back and down. There was no longer need to conserve ammo.

We heard the helicopter before we saw it again. It popped up from behind a nearby hill and came skimming in low like a giant green insect. MARINES was painted on its tail. I felt like cheering as the bird flared and hovered just above the stumps of trees. One Marine door gunner leaped out to help us while the second kept up covering fire with his machine gun. Green tracers continued to crisscross the clearing. Some penetrated the helicopter.

I was the last man to tumble into the chopper's belly. I crouched at the door and fired into the jungle as the chopper plucked the trapped patrol from the jaws of death and bit off chunks of sky with its blades. It gained altitude, circled. Just before it nosed down with speed and started south toward Da Nang, away from the Valley of the Shadow of Death, I heard a hollow pounding sound rising from the earth below.

The drums were not nearly as terrifying from an altitude of three thousand feet.

# Chapter 16

OCCASIONALLY THE TORRENTIAL DOWNPOUR of the monsoon rains thinned out to a weeping drizzle, but the relief never lasted long. The momentum of the wet season kept the low dark clouds scudding in and pouring out their heavy contents full force. Rice paddies filled and backed up the canals, which in turn backed up to flood rivers and streams. The villagers built their little towns with the rains in mind; the hamlets on their higher ground became islands in a sea of shit-brown water. The only way to move around to keep the war going was either by helicopter or by round basket boats woven by local fishermen. Marines called the boats LRDBs—"Little Round Dink Boats."

Weeks had passed—how many I didn't know, as time had little meaning anymore—since the ambush by the canebrake, but the punji hole in my leg remained as angry and threatening as the skies and kept seeping fluids. Each day in the temple at Mieu Dong when I took off the battle dressing to douse the wound with bacitracin, I threw my head aside to keep the stench out of my nostrils. Furious red streaks had erupted up my leg and the ankle was so swollen that I hobbled when I walked. Constant immersion in water wasn't helping the healing process.

"Numbah ten, numbah ten," Sergeant Nguyen Hai said, making a face. "Ro-bear, leg come off."

"It won't come off," I replied stubbornly, but I knew I was going to have to turn myself in to the company dispensary if I ever got relieved of CAC duty with the ARVNs.

Relief was not soon coming. The war was picking up, despite the rain. Marines and ARVN alike were called upon almost daily to meet the VC somewhere in the TAOR (Tactical Area of Responsibility). Intel said more and more NVA troops were pouring in from Hanoi and that Russia was supplying the VC with weapons and ammo. All we knew for sure was that the VC were fighting back in force more frequently; they didn't fire a few shots and scatter like they had right after the Marines landed. Sometimes they pinned down full companies of Marines using automatic weapons and mortars. You couldn't count on any patrol being a walk through any more.

I received orders with the ARVN at Mieu Dong to link up in a joint operation with Marine companies in a sweep from Hill 55 southwest of Da Nang to the outer perimeter of the airbase.

"I will stay and hear the radios," Tee Wee Van decided, still barefooted and still in his hammock. He looked like he had had a rough night before with his girlfriend.

I shrugged.

"Tee Wee Van numbah ten—how you say?—asshole," Sergeant Nguyen said, and we both laughed. Weeks of patrolling and the exceptional support the little veteran provided on the Hai Van had forged a strong bond between us. By now, to his amusement, I sometimes referred to him as my Gunga Din.

Nguyen Hai, myself, and ten Rangers—without their ducks and chickens—were waiting outside the temple walls when the Marine chopper came in low beneath the clouds, just above the tree line, and flared out on the LZ. The crew chief behind his M-60 machine gun in the door watched indifferently as I helped the short Vietnamese into the Sikorsky's big belly by grabbing their web gear and shoving. I banged my sore leg on the side of the chopper getting in myself and sat wrapped around it in pain as the bird lifted off again with a downroar of churned air. The fierce temple dragons glared, and then they were below and behind as the earth fell away.

I had seen Hill 55 from the air before. It resembled a withered gook tit rising out of the surrounding terrain, but it bulbed up high enough and flat enough across the top to accept several helicopters in an assault wave. Plans called for my ARVN chopper to link up in the air with chopperfuls of Marines to form an assault against the hill. Word had it that the LZ was hot.

My ARVNs' eyes were wide in the belly of the chopper. They got wider when we took ground fire and blue green tracers started slicing by outside the open door.

I watched, mesmerized, as the tracers climbed from the ground, almost lazily, looking as though they could not possibly miss, picking up speed by an illusionary process until they seemed to veer off at the last moment in a strange curve that zipped past in a streak of color. The machine gunner swiveled the barrel of his M-60 and began ripping off bursts, sending in reply streams of curving red tracers plunging into the green jungle directly below. Empty brass and belt links flew around inside the chopper. Helpless, all we could do was watch the duel and wait.

Terrified Rangers banged the butts of their weapons on the deck in unison and began chanting to bolster their flagging courage: *"Numbah ten . . . Numbah ten . . . Numbah ten."*

The pilots thought the banging was hits from ground machine gun fire. They banked evasively. The machine gunner let up on his trigger and shouted into his helmet mike. Suddenly, I became aware of a new sound—or, rather, the lack of one sound and the commencement of another. The big whining engine had quit, and now wind whistled by outside the door. Everything was much more quiet inside the machine. I had the sensation of falling, much like when a fast elevator suddenly drops out from under you. The ARVNs grabbed each other and held on, their eyes bugging.

I figured the pilots had cut the engine to get down low fast to avoid the antiaircraft barrage. I began to reassess that consideration when the machine gunner, looking alarmed, strapped himself into his seat. He kept shouting into his mike. I glanced outside. The ground rushed up as the bird swooped toward it in a fast engine-off circle. Wind howled by the door.

Involuntarily, every muscle in my body tensed and I automatically drew up my legs.

*Pull it up! Pull it up!*

We were going to land like a falling brick pile. The flooded earth was a blur of brown and green. I braced myself. The Rangers squeezed their eyelids together.

The bird hit with a tremendous splash and a jolt that tumbled me backward into the Vietnamese soldiers, all but knocking the wind from me. Arms and legs and weapons and packs were tangled up in the middle of the helicopter cargo belly like a living mass of worms.

I quickly disentangled myself. The first thing you learned to do when a chopper landed was to un-ass the damned thing. It became a tempting target on the ground. The bird was still settling, listing dangerously to the side, when I bailed out the door—and sank in water up to my chest.

"Christ!"

The machine gunner was back on his gun. The weapon swept back and forth above my head in tense jerky movements, but it was not firing. The chopper listed even more, throwing the gunner against his M-60 mount. That prompted a mass exit by the frightened ARVNs, who came sailing out the door yelling and holding their noses and windmilling their rifles. I grappled for Nguyen Hai with one hand when he came hurtling out and sank in water over his head. I brought him up sputtering and gasping for air.

The chopper's blades were slowly winding down, their

tips skimming the water on the low side. Water rippling away sounded loud in the absence of engine noise.

"Mac, your pilots picked one hell of an LZ," I shouted at the door gunner.

"LZ?" the gunner yelled back. "We auto rotated in. Marine, we've just been shot down!"

I blinked.

Getting shot down might have been my lucky day. By the time another chopper flew out to take us the rest of the way, the Marines had landed on Hill 55 and were getting the shit kicked out of them. The VC had pre-registered the hilltop as a target for mortar and heavy machine gun fire.

The fight was still going on, but not as furiously as at the beginning, when we arrived scooting down a valley and then popping up fast to slick in. The pilots did not hang around on a hot LZ. I had to bodily throw my Rangers into the new bird when it came, and now I had to throw them out again. The new crew chief sprayed the surrounding tree lines with his M-60, shooting with one hand, while with the other hand he waved frantically for us to un-ass his craft. Green tracers pierced the machine, sounding like hail stones. I glimpsed glass in the cockpit spidering and one of the pilots was looking back at us through sunglasses. He yelled something.

As soon as we were on the ground, running bent over for cover through elephant grass, the H-34 lunged forward and lifted its tail while its blades clawed so desperately for altitude that they had to have left scars on the sky. I glimpsed three Marines running toward the woods with the body of a fourth suspended among them in a poncho. The poncho and the Marines were blood-soaked. Another Marine, a blond kid who looked not to have been in-country long, lay trembling behind a clump of rocks and weeds. Eyes the size of plates turned on my ARVNs; the Marine flinched and started to bring his rifle around. I skidded down next to him. ARVNs hit the ground around us.

"They're with me!" I shouted.

117

"They're gooks," he said with a suspicious tremor in his voice.

"Good gooks. ARVN."

He still looked uncertain. "You sure?"

"Trust me, lad."

It was a helluva day. Within the past hour we had been shot out of the sky, rescued, and then injected into the middle of a firefight. What next?

I looked around to see what was going on. All I could determine was that we were in a tall grass clearing on a hilltop surrounded by sparse forest, from which the VC were laying down a withering fire. Not far away, between us and the tree line, a crater had been blown into the soil. At the bottom of it huddled a lieutenant and a radioman. The lieutenant kept talking rapidly into the radio mike while his radioman with the set on his back squatted on his heels like a monkey and kept his eyes glued to the edges of the crater, as though he expected to be overrun by gooks at any minute. Mortar explosions walked across the clearing, shredding the earth and sending shrapnel and mud whistling through the air.

We were in the open. I was going to have to do something fast. The only cover was in the tree line. I yelled at the Rangers to scatter out so one round wouldn't get us all. They started crawling on their bellies.

"What happened?" I asked the scared blond Marine.

Talking seemed to calm him. He touched my arm as gently as though touching a rose. His breathing became more controlled.

"They hit us with everything," he said hoarsely. "Mortars. Machine guns. We've taken part of the woods over there now, but you have to run across that opening to get there. There must be six or seven dead Marines. The lieutenant had us carry them to the woods. We got direct hits on us, man. Jesus! You never saw nothing like it. You could have picked up some of the Marines in their helmets."

Things looked bad, but I felt pretty good. Even the little furry creature in my guts was still. My luck was holding. After all, if the helicopter hadn't gone down when it did, we would have been on the first wave and it might have been *me* they were scooping up in a helmet. I was beginning to think I might make it out after all.

Before I had to do anything to jeopardize my troops, the lieutenant in the crater called in support. We waited and watched, keeping our heads down, while Huey gunships growled in over the horizon and worked on the surrounding tree lines with M-60s. It was an awesome display of machines and firepower. Swaths of jungle vanished. Smoke curled up toward the sky as chattering guns from the airborne platforms hurled death at the VC.

The VC weren't fools. They had hit us and hit us hard. Now they withdrew quickly and silently, once again ghosts. The choppers departed, leaving the hilltop smoking but silent. Medevac helicopters started coming in to evacuate the dead and wounded. Officers reorganized their commands in an attempt to pursue the enemy.

It was a futile pursuit. By late afternoon an uneventful sweep reached the edge of the Da Nang enclave. I slogged along in the rain, limping, and collapsed underneath a tree outside An Trach. I heard Sergeant Nguyen herding the Rangers out of a rice paddy and along the trail that slithered through the village toward my tree.

I was almost too exhausted to look up when I heard giggling. Wiping rainwater from my eyes, blinking, I glanced up in time to catch one of the Rangers crawling up over a dike. A delighted set of white teeth gleamed through the mud. The other ARVN held their sides and burst into peals of giggling and laughter.

I couldn't help myself. Maybe I was delirious. I threw my head back toward the weeping clouds and roared so hysterically I thought I must have gone insane. A squad of Marines struggling miserably by looked at us tumbling around laughing in the mud and kept on going, puzzled.

They didn't see anything funny about a Vietnamese Ranger, caked in mud from head to toe, nothing but his eyes and teeth clean, clutching a duck quacking and struggling for its life.

# Chapter 17

FIVE MONTHS. It seemed like five *years* ago that Hotel Company, unblooded and untested, crossed the Phong Le Bridge for our first taste of combat at Duong Son. I had been at Mieu Dong with Sergeant Nguyen Hai and the Rangers, it seemed, for at least half that time. It surprised me when I got orders to return to Mike Company to realize that I was actually going to miss the little Vietnamese soldiers, Nguyen most of all.

I stuffed my poncho into my packboard and I was ready to go. Nguyen Hai came into the temple with his fierce face downcast.

"It was good, Ro-bear, to fight VC with you," he said, adding with almost a whisper, *"Mon ami."*

"And with you, too," I said, adding, "Gunga Din."

We grinned at each other and clasped hands and I was gone. Tee Wee Van lifted a limp hand in farewell from his hammock and then fell back in exhaustion. It was tough work being a tee wee in a hammock.

I caught a "chicken bus" with wire mesh over the win-

121

dows to keep out grenades and got off in a dreary, steady rain where black steel girders spanned the Da Nang River. While I was gone, someone had moved the platoon's pin on the map and it had been assigned to guard the Phong Le Bridge against saboteurs. It seemed fitting. It was almost like returning home. This was where it all began, where we first crossed the river.

Highway One crossed the main bridge and continued down the coast. A muddy road just to the other side of the big bridge cut off to the southwest along an old railroad embankment and crossed the two other, smaller bridges that spanned tributaries of the river. This road curved past Duong Son and was the only dry resupply route to Third Battalion's forward headquarters.

The VC knew that.

The three bridges were well within sight of each other during daylight; it was only at night that they became isolated. I found Sergeant Shireman and Lieutenant Rowe where they had set up the platoon CP in a bunker next to an ARVN outpost by the road. O'Brien and Frenchy and the others had already spotted me and were calling out and waving from all three bridges.

Sergeant Shireman gave me his John Wayne grin as I walked up. All he needed to complete the picture was a wide Stetson hat.

"What the fuck you limping for, Roberts?"

"Sarge, I'm a wounded combat by-God Marine."

"Shit. That little punji stake hole? Goddamn, Roberts, you're getting your Purple Heart. You can stop pussing around now."

Lieutenant Rowe shook my hand. "Welcome home, Marine," he said in his soft voice. "Better see Doc Lindstrom about that leg."

First Squad had the main bridge, Weber's squad had the third bridge, which left my squad with the middle bridge, or Bridge Two. Squad leader Corporal Bob Bellot pointed out the squad members' positions on the bridge.

"Ekstein's crew is at the other end of the bridge. Yates

122

and Smitty are here with me. You can link up with Leslie and O'Brien across the road. You'll be with Bruce again when he gets back from the airbase."

I started across the road to the sandbagged hootches. There were sandbag emplacements on all four corners of the bridge.

"Roberts?"

I paused. Bellot resembled a tank, low-slung and broad with enough muscle to bust through a concrete bunker. He liked to run point on patrol with a cocked .45 auto in one hand and a frag grenade with the pin pulled in the other. That way, he said, if the gooks got him he'd be ready to take some of them with him.

"Don't get too comfortable," he said. "You're on watch next."

He grinned.

"Welcome home, Roberts."

Waiting was the name of the game at the bridges. Time merged and had no meaning. Rain kept the surface of the rice paddies dimpling. Grayness settled over the land and into our soggy souls. Every day, the water rose until the land that remained was like islands in a delta. The grayline between sky and flooded land became difficult to distinguish. We stood our watches with rainwater dribbling off our helmets, our feet squishing in wet boots. We caught crotch rot and sneezes on top of dysentery and parasites and foot rot.

O'Brien's poncho leaked where he had spread it over a circle of sandbags.

"Ain't no Arab in the history of Arabs ever had to endure this shit," he said. "Arabs are desert people."

He strode back and forth on the bridge loudly voicing his displeasure to the lowering clouds.

"Jee-suz Kee-rist, we are sitting-fucking-ducks. The gooks can sneak a boat up on us anytime they want. Boom!"

Pete Yates was on watch, looking miserable. "Why don't you talk a little louder and tell 'em about it, you dumb fuck?" he suggested.

O'Brien stopped and looked around. "Jee-suz Kee-rist,

Yates. You ain't afraid of a few dinks, are you, buddy? We'll turn 'em into a pink mist so quick they'll become their own ancestors.''

O'Brien's was a common worry: that the gooks would swim up at night and mine the bridges with us on them. To prevent it—or at least to slow them down—we constructed apron-string entanglement fences by driving fence posts deep into the soft earth on either end and either side of the bridges and stretching double strands of barbed wire underwater across the streams. We wove steel barbed wire and concertina into these strands to make underwater entanglement even a carp would think twice about swimming through. We added claymore mines above the wire, camouflaged them with water grasses, and ran the firing clackers up to the emplacements at the ends of the bridges.

Then we waited some more.

Headquarters was worried about infiltrators and mines and sappers hitting the airfield. At the bridges, our worries were a bit more fundamental. The main concern of the bridge watch was dysentery.

Vietnam meant the shits. Wherever you were when the urge struck, you dropped your pants. There was no stemming the tide. Some grunt would come tearing out of his hootch in the middle of a rainstorm, hooting and hollering to clear the path. Sometimes he made it to the end of the bridge, sometimes he didn't. A sheepish grin told of his success, or lack of it. At Counter-guerrilla Warfare School in Okinawa, instructors warned us that the VC could smell our cologne a mile away. After the first few weeks in-country, you didn't have to worry about cologne. You gave the VC something stronger to smell.

Engineers tried to help by purifying drinking water for us in big open rubber tanks on the bank of the river next to the main bridge. The chemicals they used burned the throat. I asked one of the engineers if there wasn't a way of purifying water without turning it into gasoline.

"You know how many germs, bacterias, and amoebas there are in this stuff?'' the engineer asked.

I eyed the rubber tanks. "No."

"Millions . . . goddamned *millions*," he said, dumping a bucketful of chemicals into a tank.

"Know where we get this water?" he continued.

Hoses ran from pumps to the water's edge. "The river."

"Know where the river gets its water?"

"From the streams and canals?"

"Know where the streams and canals get their water?"

What was this—Twenty Questions?

"From the rain?"

"It rains in the rice paddies and the rice paddies overflow into the streams and canals," the engineer said. "What are the paddies fertilized with?"

"Shit. Human shit."

The engineer grinned and jabbed a finger at the canteens on my web gear.

"You," he concluded, "are carrying two canteens full of shit and chlorine."

And Kool-Aid. Thank God for Kool-Aid.

Mail call was the big social event of the day. Going down the road to battalion HQ to pick up the platoon's mail was almost as good as getting mail yourself. It broke up the boredom by giving you a chance to circulate and see how the war was going elsewhere. We would have fought for the privilege if the squad leaders had not split up the opportunity. Hitching a ride on the next vehicle was equivalent in the real world to a ride and a picnic in the country.

When it was my turn, I prolonged the experience by walking around the HQ compound talking to Marines from other companies and platoons. I limped past a couple of 81mm mortar pits where the crews were preparing their tubes for a fire mission. I stopped to watch.

"Getting ready for tonight?" I ventured.

One of the crewmen looked up. "Naw," he said. "We're going to lob some rounds at the ARVNs over in their camp."

I stared. "ARVNs?"

"The zipperheads laid a few on us last night. The gook commander said it was an accident."

I thought of the friendly fire at Cam Ne. "Maybe it was."

"Three nights in a row? The ol' man wants them to see what happens when you fuck with the Marines. This ain't the Army."

It was a fucked-up war.


Second Platoon had been suffering casualties almost from the time we crossed the Phong Le Bridge for the first time. Cam Ne had taken its toll, as had punji stakes and booby traps and snipers and the shits. The shits dried you up. The shits could kill you the same as a fruit jar mine on a bamboo gate.

Down now to two-thirds strength, the platoon had not received a single replacement since we stormed ashore on China Beach to kids and old women selling Cokes. That was why the lone stranger who dropped off the six-by at Bridge One on an afternoon created so much excitement. He checked in with Lieutenant Rowe and then came walking up the road toward Bridge Two. Even from a distance you could tell he wore fresh Stateside utilities. As he drew nearer, you could almost see a starch crease. His hair, by God, hadn't even grown back from boot camp.

"Wha' the fuck?" Dave Bruce wondered, standing in the middle of the bridge to get a better look.

The field phone rang. I was on watch.

"Roberts? Ekstein here. You ain't gonna believe this. We actually got some new meat."

Bellot's squad ganged up on the end of the bridge to wait for the newby, our first. The private was a skinny kid wearing glasses. He looked scared and he hadn't even been shot at yet. He advanced with a halting gait that finally abandoned him altogether and left him standing staring uncertainly back at the rough-looking bunch that waited to either greet him or throw him off the bridge, he couldn't tell which.

"Get your ass on up here, lad," Corporal Bellot called.

He came on up. "Sir, I'm Private Raglund, sir."

"I ain't no 'sir,' Raglund. I'm Corporal Bellot. Where you from?"

That was always asked.

"Seattle, Washington, Corporal."

I edged forward, curious. "You're the first replacement we've gotten," I said. "How did you end up in Vietnam?"

The kid ducked his head to hide behind his glasses.

"I kinda went AWOL on boot camp leave," he confessed.

"Ain't that kinda like being pregnant?" O'Brien asked. "You either are or you ain't."

Raglund gave us a sheepish half-grin. "Anyhow, the FBI caught me and I ended up in the brig. I was there for a couple of months until the next thing I knew, the guards took me out one morning and said I got orders to go overseas. They didn't tell me it was Vietnam."

Bellot studied him for a second. "Keep your nose clean, Raglund," he said at last. "Ain't no place to go AWOL over here anyhow except Dog Patch—and I don't think you got the balls for that."

Smitty sneered. "Welcome to the asshole of the world, Raglund."

The platoon got probed that night. VC cracked off a few shots from a tree line across the paddies west of Bridge Two. It was almost a welcome relief from the boredom. I sent up a parachute flare. The M-60 machine gun from Bridge One arced a stream of tracers toward the tree line. Everybody got in a little trigger time until the squad leaders started yelling to "Cease fire, goddamnit!"

The new guy tucked himself in beside me behind the sandbags, hugging the bridge planking. Moonlight—rare for this time of year—reflected in his glasses.

"Is . . . is this a firefight?" he stammered.

I looked at him.

"This ain't shit," I said. "I'll let you know when we have a firefight."

From the bridges we kept hearing reports of more frequent contacts with ever-increasing numbers of Viet Cong and

NVA. Americans were being hit harder all over South Vietnam. The enemy was getting bolder. LBJ kept building up our troops and Uncle Ho kept building up his.

"It keeps on like this," Sergeant Shireman predicted, "and we'll have us a *real* little war over here."

"Sar-jun, it ees almost Christmas," Frenchy pointed out.

The sergeant grinned, looking more hawkish than ever. "Merry Christmas, Frenchy. Now, go waste gooks."

ARVN soldiers might not have been the best fighters around, but they were enterprising, you had to hand them that. One of them, who owned his own jeep, of which he was justly proud—"It's probably stole," O'Brien decided—made a deal with laundresses in Dog Patch to come around to the Marine outposts to pick up soiled laundry and deliver the clean. It was a good deal for everyone.

One morning after he made his drop-off and pick-up and started off down the road, the platoon was shocked by a tremendous explosion that picked up the ARVN's jeep and hurled it upside down into the flooded rice paddy. One wheel continued to revolve slowly above the water. A column of black smoke rose from the road between Bridges Two and Three, next to which the green-uniformed body of the Vietnamese soldier lay face down looking like so much soiled laundry.

Our worst fears were realized. With us constantly on guard, the VC had nevertheless managed to sneak up and mine the road. What could prevent them from mining the bridges? From then on we patrolled the roads between and the engineers came out every day and swept with mine detectors.

O'Brien scratched his head when a chopper came out to haul off the dead ARVN.

"Wonder who we can get to do our laundry now?" he said.

The VC, it seemed, were multiplying like rats in a sewer. They even took to hitting us in the daytime, something that would have been unthinkable a few months ago. The war had progressed a long way from crossbow traps and solitary riflemen with WWII surplus weapons. It kept escalating. They fired at us with bolt-action rifles and we shot back at them with automatic weapons; they went to automatic and we zapped them with machine guns; they tried machine guns and we switched to artillery. They were starting to strike us with squads and platoons and even companies armed with the latest Soviet and Chicom weapons.

We hated them for it—the dinks, the gooks, the zipper-heads. It was their fault. They were keeping us over here. Frenchy was the only one among us by this time to hold any hopes, and he held them only out of desperation, that the war, if not over by Christmas, would most certainly start winding down by Easter or by July Fourth at the latest.

"July Fourth, zee Independence Day—*that* would be a good day," he said.

O'Brien put a damper on that. "Sergeant Shireman said Christmas. Only, he didn't say which Christmas."

"Christmas 1980," Leslie said gloomily.


Huey gunships, summoned in response to enemy riflemen in the tree line, came *whop-whopping* over the rainy horizon from the airbase. They looked like evil green insects with stingers of pylon-mounted M-60 machine guns and 2.75-inch rocket pods. It was going to be a good show. We lined the bridges to watch the first ship as it scooted across the paddy so low its blades kicked up a misty typhoon of water. It sidled sideways along the tree line, like a nearsighted mantis peering for its prey.

It flushed out a gook who, either too excited or too foolish to run for it, stood up and began firing point-blank at the bird. All six of the chopper's M-60s opened up in a deafening burst that went on and on and vibrated the helicopter in the air. Smoke swirled. The gook literally exploded.

The audience on the bridges cheered and applauded. It *was* a good show.

That Huey nosed over and took a running start before it

climbed high in a bank. Its wing mate swooped in on-target, linked to the tree line by rocket contrails. Eruptions in the jungle felled trees. Smoke billowed, expanded, and floated lazily away toward Da Nang.

We cheered again and let off a few rounds of our own at the trees. The Huey pilot laughed over the radio.

"You grunts owe us a beer," he said.

I thought when I left the temple at Mieu Dong that I might not see Sergeant Nguyen Hai and his BDQs anymore, but the war around the Da Nang TAOR was a small war. We had been slogging back and forth across the area for months; it had become as familiar to us as our own blocks back home. Nguyen Hai made a point of diverting his patrols past the bridges.

We were standing one day in the road, chatting about "old times" and leaning on our weapons, when snipers opened up on the bridge watch from the same tree line the Hueys had worked over before. Same chapter, same page, different verse. We got down behind the bridge embankment and cautiously stuck up our heads to have a look at Leslie and Bellot exchanging fire with the gooks. Nguyen pointed out a faint trace of smoke in the trees.

"Hai see VC," he said calmly.

"Have your BAR open up on him," I suggested.

The BAR gunner had been on the patrol to the Valley of the Shadow of Death. He grinned as he set the gun on bipods and laid on the trigger. The gun chattered. Smoke swirled. Marine M-14s joined the chorus.

Corporal Bellot tanked across the bridge, keeping down in a low, fast profile. Right behind him ran Balla, a quiet, stocky kid who did just what he was told and no more.

"Roberts—take Balla with you. Try to get over there and flank the slant-eyed bastards before they get away."

Balla and Nguyen Hai followed as I led the way in a run using the embankment for cover. Farther down, we crossed over at a point out of sight of the enemy and waded the edge of the rice paddies until we reached the tree line at the opposite end from the snipers. The little patrol pushed into the wet darkness of the forest and made its way through it slowly. Tracers from the bridge marked the gooks' position.

The little creature in my gut was awake, but it wasn't clawing; it was intent like a predator stalking.

When we were close to the snipers but still far enough away not to be seen by them through the jungle, I stepped into the open and waved my arms at the bridges. The firing ceased. I heard a distant dog barking. I heard my own breathing. Some of the Marines on the bridges stood up from behind cover to watch the drama's final act. It was foolish, as the VC, like the bamboo viper, were deadly until they were dead.

We edged forward through the jungle, stalking, halting every few steps to strain our ears.

I heard rustling sounds in the bushes to my right. In this business, if you were slow you were dead. I whirled toward the sound, along with Nguyen. Balla was momentarily out of sight to the left.

Rustling again. A stealthy footstep. We opened fire.

Nguyen's Thompson and my M-14 cut a thunderous swath out of the jungle undergrowth. Bushes exploded, but I kept firing, slapping in another magazine when the first was finished, and firing some more, as though by sheer volume we could ensure that the enemy did not return fire.

Then there was some more silence. I was panting. Fighting did that to you. Sweat stung my eyes. Nguyen did not take his eyes nor his weapon off the place of danger, but from the corner of my eye I saw him nod. His fierce face resembled that of a hunting tiger. Balla came running up, but he said nothing, just kept sweeping the jungle around with his rifle, tense and ready.

I pointed into the bushes and signaled that we spread out. Balla moved to one side. We started carefully forward, fingers on triggers.

Ten meters deeper into the bush we came upon the bodies. Two of them, bloody and torn and grotesque, twisted on top of each other, like pieces of freshly killed beef contaminated with shreds of black cloth. It was the first time I had actually gotten a close look at someone I had killed. Curiously fascinated, I edged forward.

Water dripped from the overhanging branches into an upturned face. It took a minute before I recognized the features with the wide-staring eyes. Nguyen Hai recognized the dead man at the same time. Papers from the body identified him as a Viet Cong officer. The scar at the edge of Nguyen's mouth crinkled as a grin slid slowly across his face. He remembered an arrogant little government man who had insisted we follow him into the Viet Cong's lair.

The dead sniper was none other than the government rice tax collector. I wondered what he had done, officer that he was, to end up like a private sniping at Marines, unless he was just out having a little sport.

I grinned, too. It was worth grinning about.


VC kept filtering into and through the TAOR, like rats that infest an old and decaying house no matter how many traps or how much poison you put out to destroy them. A few nights after we killed the tax collector, near midnight, Bridge One rang Bridge Two on the field phone. Bruce and I were on watch. I stood drowsily propped against the sandbag emplacement, while Bruce leaned across the bridge railing staring at the water we could hear below lapping at stanchions.

I picked up the clacking phone. Frenchy's voice came across the headset tense and businesslike, devoid of its normal good-natured banter.

"Get everyone up," he said.

"What's going on?"

"There ees sheet everywhere. The dinks are hitting MAG-16. The skipper thinks that ees a diversion and that zee gooks will try for the airbase. We are on one hundred percent alert."

If they went for the airbase, they'd first try to cut off reinforcements from the field battalions by knocking out the bridges. It appeared we might be the pivot in a major gook operation.

By the time I got the squad up, the night sky to the east had lit up with fireworks. It looked like the MAG-16 helicopter base located at the foot of Marble Mountain was ablaze. Poor fuckers. They were taking a lot of shit. Bellot and the squad lined the bridge railing in full combat gear to wonder and speculate. There was the nervous sound of weapons being checked, magazines loaded and locked.

"Jee-suz Kee-rist."

That was good enough for all of us.

We watched until Pete Yates hissed from across the road where he was keeping watch.

"I got movement," he said.

The squad went instantly alert, spreading out. Bellot ran to Yates where he crouched inside the sandbag bunker, pointing.

"Straight out across the paddies," Yates went on. "Looks like they're trying to get around us to get at Bridge One."

I rang Bridge One to warn Sergeant Shireman. Bellot filled the sky with parachute flares. The weird brilliant suns floating high overhead, descending slowly, trapped a short file of black-clad men attempting to sneak along a dike between our bridge and Sergeant Shireman's. The squad pinned the gooks down with a rattle of rifle fire. Bridge One opened up on them in a crossfire. The gooks returned lead the best they could, but most of the green tracers flew wild.

This firefight was still raging when the third bridge let loose in a different direction.

"The fuckers are everywhere!" O'Brien yelled.

I emptied a magazine and was slapping in a fresh one when Raglund crawled up to the row of sandbags.

"Is . . . is *this* a firefight?" he wanted to know, sounding as though, if it weren't, he did not want to be around when there was one.

"This is a firefight," I shouted back, springing up to let off another burst. I glanced at Raglund cowering on his belly. "Care to join us?"

The bridges were not directly attacked, although infiltrators kept trying to sneak past toward the airfield until dawn. Everyone in the TAOR was kept busy that night. A squad from India Company ambushed a large element of VC near a village called An Tu, about a mile south of the bridges. We heard the clatter of their fire. The enemy left fifteen KIAs behind, which meant the body count must have been easily twice that, considering the VC penchant for carrying off their casualties.

We heard firing coming from every direction until shortly before dawn. Then it slacked off as the VC took to their holes. News began to trickle in. The enemy had got in its licks, too. Nineteen helicopters had been destroyed and thirty-four others damaged at MAG-16. Marines had been killed, but no one was saying how many. The new Naval hospital across the road from MAG-16 burned all night, glowing against the horizon like a rising sun.

The VC offensive continued at nightfall the next day when enemy waves attacked the First Battalion, First Marines, entrenched on Hill 22. After Action reports listed sixteen Marines KIA'd and forty-one WIA'd. The enemy body count left behind numbered forty-seven.

It was a war of attrition. Sergeant Shireman was right. It *was* becoming a *real* war.

# Chapter 18

Hᴏᴡ ᴄᴏᴜʟᴅ Vɪᴇᴛɴᴀᴍ not create paranoia? Whenever people were not sneaking around trying to kill you, you were sneaking around trying to kill them. It gave you a fatalistic attitude. It was not as bad to be killed today if you were playing the game and had nothing better going tomorrow, as it was if you were expecting something like R & R or rotation home. Expecting something made you more careful. It also made you fearful that, at the last moment, fate would turn against you.

Tense and unsmiling, the Marines who filed aboard the big C-130 Hercules and strapped themselves into the webbing knew absolutely that something would happen to ground the R & R taxi to Okinawa. Like a VC attack or an engine malfunction. Dressed out in khakis that had stayed folded in the bottom of a seabag in storage at Da Nang since my arrival in Vietnam, I watched the tail ramp close, blocking my view of the familiar tent cities and temporary buildings at the airbase. I listened to the big engines roar. The aircraft lurched, throwing us against seatbelts. It started to move.

It was not until the nose lifted and the cargo plane climbed above Da Nang, circled once, and then set a course out to sea toward Okinawa that the Marines cheered mightily and sank back with relief.

As I was the first in the platoon to draw out-of-country R & R, the others extracted a promise that I would return and provide a blow-by-blow account. A combat Marine on R & R—Rest and Relaxation, Rape and Ruin—was supposed to get "screwed, blued, and tattooed." I owed it to my buddies who stayed behind to R & R for them, too. Party hardy. Raise hell.

Before I left, O'Brien, amidst laughter, warned that I might not return, that some slant-eye in Okinawa would bed me and wed me and I'd do like Raglund and go AWOL.

"Get fucked," O'Brien advised. "Lose your virginity, Roberts, but don't get fucked up."

Looking like a skeleton of what I had been six months ago, old and weary and worn-out at nineteen, I hobbled onto the plane at Da Nang and hobbled off it in Okinawa. At Doc Lindstrom's advice, I had gone to the company medic about my wound, but he gave me some more bacitracin and sent me back.

Camp Hague in Okinawa had an R & R officer who met us when we got off the airplane. A typical REMF—Rear Echelon Mother-Fucker—who made no bones about his desire to stay that way, he was of the type who tailored his uniform, wore spit-shined shoes, and went around on a short neck with his jaw stuck out. He took one look at our uniforms mildewed by the wet climate of Vietnam and lifted a lip as though he had just found a turd in his lunch.

"Your uniforms look like shit," he said. "You will buy civilian clothes before you will be allowed off the base."

Shitbird.

Okinawans had lined up their peddlar carts outside on the street, waiting, bowing and smiling in that way that meant they knew the routine and had you on the hook. I filed quietly out with the others, still feeling numb from the rapid transition from war zone to this, and made a selection from clothing stacked on the carts. All the shirts were white and the trousers black, like the now-dead tax collector wore on our rounds that day. I hung a white shirt and black pants on my skinny frame. The only pair of shoes I could find—black, of course—were two sizes too large.

I looked like Charlie Chaplin. We all did. The R & R officer nodded his approval.

I ended up in a topless bar in Koza trying to get screwed, blued, and tattooed for my buddies. A girl wearing bikini bottoms and pasties with tassles pranced out on a low runway and began to shake and gyrate. Her tassles swirled like propellers. I peered at them—and then drank some more beer. Charlie Chaplin getting drunk in a sleazy bar. I drank and peered and decided I knew what was wrong.

"She ain't got no tits," I declared.

No one heard me.

"She ain't got no tits," I shouted.

"Hey, fella, shut up."

"She's supposed to dance topless and she's wearing those little swirly things on her tits."

"Better watch it, fella, or they'll throw your ass in jail for drunk."

I thought about it. So what if they threw me in jail. At least I'd be in Okinawa with clean sheets and a roof that didn't leak.

*"She ain't got no tits."*

"Fella!"

*"No tits."*

I was looking for a fight. The dogface doing all the talking regarded me from across the barroom for a minute. The white shirt and black pants told where I had been as surely as though I had walked in wearing a helmet and flak jacket. The doggie turned his back to me.

"Fuck you, fella," he said.

I had to have the last word. "That's what I want—a fuck."

"Why didn't you say so? Here—let me tell you where to go."

I caught a skoshi cab that drove along a winding road

overlooking the sea and dropped me off in front of a geisha house out in the country. A flatfaced older woman in a kimono served tea and cakes in a rice straw bowl. Afterward, she led me by the hand to a small green-tiled room where I stripped and took a steam bath. Two young girls also in kimonos came in giggling and dried me with large, rough towels. All over they dried me. They had great asses. My eyes followed their asses like a pair of poodles with their tongues out.

Wait until I got back and told O'Brien and the others.

"You got tits," I said.

Still tittering, the girls helped me onto a table where they went to work massaging weary muscles. When they came to my leg, they recoiled with a cacophony of little cries.

"Ooooh . . . numbah ten. How you get?"

"Viet Cong . . . in Vietnam."

"Ooooooh! No *ichi-ban.*"

They wouldn't look at the wound from then on. They sprinkled me with talcum powder, all except for the leg. The scent made me think briefly of Rita and the bottle of perfume, but I dismissed such thoughts because they made me ache. Instead, I lay belly down, still a little drunk, and ran through a riot of fantasies about what I would tell the platoon when I got back.

*No shit, there I was, O'Brien . . . Two of them with the nicest little asses . . .*

*Roberts, you ain't gonna tell me you fucked both of them?*

*Not exactly at the same time.*

*But you did it to 'em?*

*Why, hell, yes.*

*Hey, Roberts is gonna tell us a fuck story. What a man!*

*There I was. I fucked one and then I got a massage—a real massage—and then I banged the other one.*

*No shit?*

*No shit.*

There was an oscillating electric fan in the room that blew cool across my naked body while the skillful girls joyfully kneaded out the tension and anxiety of a half-year in Vietnam. That was the last I remember—the wind across my back and those tiny cool hands working up and down, up and down.

I fell asleep. I wouldn't tell O'Brien that.

When I awoke the girls were gone and the room was dark. I didn't realize where I was. My little furry creature hooked his claws. I sprang off the table and was looking for my rifle before I discovered I was naked. It dawned on me then that I was in a geisha house in Okinawa, standing alone in a dark room, naked and foolish.

The mamasan came in, turned on the light, and collected for the massage and for the sake I drank.

"Hey, I didn't get any . . ."

"Too late, too late, soldier-boy. You sleep. Girls all gone. All gone. So sorry."

I found myself in short order standing outside in the darkness watching her close the door in my face. I had to have the last word.

"I ain't no fucking soldier-boy!" I shouted. "I'm a by-God U.S. Marine."

Then I hobbled away.

*No shit, there I was . . .*

# Chapter 19

THIRD BATTALION'S PIN on the map was a lucky and safe green, at least for the time being. The battalion moved back to the airbase to serve a tour as Air Base Defense Battalion. Second Platoon traded the boredom of the bridges for the boredom and drudgery of constructing a new bunker line on the airfield perimeter.

The war was turning modern. The new bunkers were prefabs. All we had to do was take eight-foot, pre-cut timbers and spike them together around holes we dug by hand and E-tool, pile sandbags around the sides and on the roofs, then move into them behind coils of concertina wire and trip flares and empty C-ration tin cans filled with pebbles so they'd rattle a warning if sappers tried to get through.

There wasn't much to be done after that, except take turns running squad-sized patrols to the nearby villages to keep the enemy at bay. Rarely did the VC come into the enclave this near the base, so we looked upon the patrols as an annoyance the brass dreamed up to keep us from getting lazy.

The Army set up a club in one of its tents and stocked it with cold beer and a juke box. Some of us ambled into it one afternoon to check it out, bellying up to a bar constructed of old ammo cases and rocket boxes. We heard our first "protest" song screaming out of the juke box:

> . . . the eastern world, it is explodin' . . .

It was called "Eve of Destruction." We listened to it in surprise and wonder. The Armed Forces Radio Service rarely told us what was going on back home. I laughed uncomfortably.

"Sounds like Vietnam," I said.

Smitty snorted and broke it down to its simplest terms: "What do them pussies know about Vietnam?"

O'Brien walked around the music machine like he considered putting a foot through it.

"Jee-suz Kee-rist," he said. "The Army ain't nothing but a bunch of commies and democrats. It's about time to bust the place up, ain't it, Roberts?"

Sergeant Shireman had already taken insurance against that. "If I catch just one of you assholes fucking with the doggies or tearing up their club," he'd growled, "I will personally cut your asshole out with my K-bar and drag your intestines all the way to Chu Lai."

The thing with Sergeant Shireman was, you *believed* him.

Mike Company was responsible for the security of the southwest corner of the airbase perimeter. During daylight hours, we manned a row of old French watchtowers just outside the electrified net fence. At night we patrolled between the fence and our concertina wire and kept watch from the bunkers.

Safely behind the fence, Air Force Police guarded the F-4 revetments and the unmarked C-46 and C-47 cargo planes belonging to Air America, the CIA airline. Every day the airplanes loaded up with heavy crates onto which were strapped cargo parachutes, and flew off into the clouds on secret missions, often returning riddled with bullet holes.

While Marines crouched in the mud outside the fence gnawing cold C-rations out of cans, jeeps on the other side of the fence brought out hot chow to the Air Force Police. The APs turned their backs on the emaciated, exhausted, and diseased combat troops outside the wire and ate real food, ignoring the taunts and catcalls. We were on the outside looking in, like stepchildren. The Marines quickly stoked up a seething resentment of the Air Police.

I hobbled over to the fence. I had had to cut the top off my boot because of the swelling of my leg. The AP nearest the fence on the other side was sitting comfortably in his jeep eating from a mess hall tray. Everything about him looked healthy. Even his uniform was in good shape.

I stared at him while he ate. Finally, he looked up. It was a quick uneasy glance before he turned his back to me and kept eating. It made me feel like a street urchin in Dog Patch with my nose pressed to a café window.

*"Fuck you!"* I shouted at the AP's back.

He kept eating, like he hadn't heard.

The Marines were either on guard taunting the APs, on patrol, or lounging around the prefab bunkers waiting to go on guard to taunt the APs or on patrol. Waiting. Like at the bridges. War was more waiting than anything else. Christmas was going to catch us on airbase perimeter watch. Looking through the fence, we could see little decorated Christmas trees springing up in officers' tents, mess tents, and the like. Some of them glowed with real colored lights that reflected in the mud outside when a tent flap opened.

I got to feeling so lonely, seeing them, that I wouldn't even look in their direction. It was like they were put there and decorated to mock us.

"It ees not going to be over by Christmas," Frenchy finally conceded.

"Sure it will," Smitty said. "Christmas, 1985."

Feeling depressed, I propped my throbbing foot up on an ammo crate outside my bunker and eased down on sandbags to brew up a canteen cup of C-rat coffee. Add a little powdered milk, sugar, and cocoa to it and it was almost as good as a milk shake. Several jets taking off from the airstrip on missions streaked across the red face of the sun before it slid behind a bank of black clouds. An AP in a jeep cruised slowly by beyond the fence and waved. I did not wave back.

Hardly had I gotten a heat tab burning underneath the canteen cup and gotten comfortable myself than I heard a shout. Looking up, I saw PFC Richard Hunt running toward me flailing his long arms and casting terrified looks over his shoulder. I couldn't see anyone chasing him. I thought he must have finally gone raving mad. It was only a matter of time until it started happening.

Hunt shot past in a blur. *"Kill it! Kill it!"* he screamed as he went by.

In hot pursuit came a snake—a long, thin, emerald green bamboo viper, as poisonous and aggressive as the Okinawan Habu. The snake seemed to be gaining.

The Marine circled my bunker.

"Goddamnit, Roberts! *Kill it!*" he bellowed the second time around.

"Fucking snake's catching me," he complained breathlessly the third time.

*"Help!"* he pleaded the fourth time when the snake showed no sign of losing either its determination or its stamina.

It was comic relief in the nick of time. I was laughing so hard I missed the snake the first swing when I finally got to my machete.

"Run him by again, Hunt," I instructed.

"Quit fucking around, Roberts," Hunt gasped. "This is serious."

"Everybody said you'd fuck a snake if somebody held its head." I laughed. "What'd you do? Get it pregnant?"

"It ain't funny, Roberts. All I did was throw a rock at it."

He kicked at the remains with the toe of his boot.

"Must be a VC snake," he said. "Think we can call in a body count on it?"

Sometimes, on airbase perimeter, you could almost forget there was a war going on on the other side of the bridge, but when you did the war had a way of reminding you.

Bellot's squad got up before dawn one morning to run a short patrol to check on a village that had reported VC activity. Grumbling and sleepy, we wended our way through the wire entanglements and came to an old mine field emplaced by the French more than fifteen years ago as part of their defenses. Engineers had cleared and marked a narrow path across the field; it shone white like a thread in the last of the starlight.

I trudged along at my interval, limping, head down, not paying much attention; crossing the minefield had become as familiar to us as our own bunkers. I saw where the trail split. We normally took the route to the left, but I thought nothing of going to the right until a terrific explosion obliterated the man ahead of me in a blinding flash of light. The surprise was comparable to sitting down to watch TV and having the set blow up in your face.

We froze with instant realization. We had somehow gotten onto the wrong path and into the minefield. Big Jan Wertz was writhing with shock and pain on the ground just ahead of me. His screams pierced the stillness of the dawn and made me forget that my own legs were stinging from pieces of shrapnel.

*"My foot . . . goddamnit, it's gone! Do you hear? My fucking foot!"*

Funny the things you remember at times like that. I remembered Wertz had played high school football in New Jersey. He was a linebacker who had offers of a scholarship when he got back from Vietnam. The pros had already been scouting him. I wondered if his foot really had gotten blown off. He was lucky if that was all he lost.

"Don't anybody move, hear?" That was Bellot from up front. His voice was steady and calming. "Just don't move.

I don't want anybody else on a mine. Keep still a minute. Who's nearest him?"

Sweat popped out on my face. I took a deep breath. "I am."

"Who's that?"

"Roberts."

"Roberts, can you get to him? I'm coming back, too. Don't anybody else move. We'll have to follow our own footprints back out when we can."

I breathed deeply, looking at Wertz and steeling myself to take that first step. My eyes scanned for footprints in the sand. If I stepped directly in them I was probably safe, unless the mines were so old they didn't go off the first or second time they were stepped on.

"How the fuck did this happen? Who the fuck was on point?"

"Shut up, Palin," Bellot snapped.

"Point needs his ass kicked for this shit—leading us into the mines."

"Just shut the fuck up, Palin."

Palin was the asshole of the squad. Nobody wanted to be around him. Tall and skinny and beady-eyed, he could always find something to bitch about. Back at Pendleton I threatened to shoot him when we got to Vietnam and make it look like the enemy did it. I was always afraid he *would* get shot and I'd get the blame. Why couldn't it have been *him* who stepped on the mine? Seemed like nothing ever happened to assholes.

I took a step. Wertz screamed. The furry creature in my gut jumped into my throat. It was a cool morning, but my shirt clung wet to my back. Sweat made the pinprick lacerations on my legs sting.

"Roberts?" Bellot inquired.

"I'm going to him."

I took another step, another, and I was almost there. So far, so good. One more step and I knelt next to him, sighing with relief. The way he was wriggling around there shouldn't be any mines left near him.

I couldn't bear to return the pleading gaze he turned on me.

"Roberts, I ain't never going to play football no more, am I?"

He was still now, bent forward at the waist on his side with both hands clutching the bloody mass at the end of his leg. Bellot joined me with his flashlight while I prepared a tourniquet. The beam revealed that Wertz's foot appeared to be missing below the ankle.

"Bob, tell me the truth," Wertz implored, but he really didn't want to know the truth. Not yet. He wanted reassurance, and neither of us could give him that.

"You're going home," Bellot evaded.

"But I can't play football."

"I don't know," Bellot lied.

If the ghosts of the present war did not get you when it was your turn, then the ghosts of a previous war did. It was a fucked-up war.

And it was a long way from over by Christmas. Frenchy said he wasn't even going to roll out of his poncho all day. "I will pretend that it ees not Christmas," he decided.

I was walking my post on guard duty between the concertina wire and the fence when a Mitey Mite pulled up in the drizzling rain. George Renninger and Tommy Shands climbed down from the French watchtower behind me, their rifles slung and their bodies hunched underneath their wet ponchos. Lieutenant Rowe billowing in his own poncho got out of the little vehicle and motioned me over, too. His driver pulled out a "vac" can and opened the lid. Inside was turkey and dressing. It smelled like something else.

"Merry fuckin' Christmas, Marines," the driver said.

"You mean we got hot chow?"

"The cooks spent all morning opening cans, but at least it's warm."

I watched the rain dilute the contents of my mess kit plate.

C-rations tasted like C-rations no matter what you did to them.

"Merry Christmas," Lieutenant Rowe said a little sadly before he got back into the Mitey Mite and it splashed away through the rain toward the next post.

Renninger looked up at the row of bunkers, the fence, the coiled wire merging into the grayness of Christmas Day, the solitary figures of helmeted warriors standing outside in the weather eating silently in the downpour. A wistful smile touched lips cracked by the sun.

"Yeah," he murmured. "Merry fuckin' Christmas."

# Chapter 20

FOR SMITTY, WITH his ability to break life down to its simplest terms, like a Missouri mule on its way to a feeding, a day's liberty meant a whorehouse, followed by a good clean fistfight with the squids or the doggies in some bar. Big as he was, he was a good man to have on your side in a fistfight.

Most of the boom-boom houses in Da Nang were off-limits to GIs, as they were rumored to be frequented as much by the VC as by Americans who went to them, off-limits or no off-limits. But what the hell, O'Brien reflected. Even the Viet Cong needed a piece of ass occasionally—and they weren't about to wear out the pussy any with their little bitty dink dicks.

"Let's get laid!" Smitty bugled.

Marine liberty uniform was khakis, bloused jungle boots, helmet liner, and M-14 rifle. O'Brien always joked that a helmet on Smitty's huge head looked like a C-ration can stretched over a watermelon. O'Brien was teasing him now as the three of us strode jauntily down Doc Lap Street.

"Jee-suz Kee-rist, Smitty. Just like you farm boys. Wanting to eat your cake first."

"I don't want to eat it—maybe just nibble around the edges a bit. I want to fuck it."

"Let's eat, then we'll get you laid."

"I want two of them—like Roberts had in Okinawa."

I still hadn't told them I went to sleep.

Smitty was all hormones with big feet. Impatiently all through water buffalo steaks and a case of beer at a place called The New Chicago Cabaret Smitty kept demanding, "When do I get laid?" The café had heavy screen mesh over the windows to keep grenades out.

Finally, O'Brien's Arab face lit up with a devilish grin and his eyes sparkled behind his glasses.

"Let's get Smitty laid."

We were uproariously drunk by then. The three of us with some difficulty squeezed our bodies into a sicylo built for two small Vietnamese. The old driver, who had a Ho Chi Minh beard and a rice straw hat, shook his head and stared uncertainly at the big towering American with the two skinny ones all but in his lap. Then he climbed confidently onto the three-wheeled bicycle.

"Number one boom-boom house," O'Brien ordered expansively.

Uncle Ho smiled. "Ahhh. You like numbah one Hong Kong boom-boom girl?"

"Numbah one, numbah one," Smitty eagerly agreed.

Two blocks later, with the elderly Vietnamese panting down our necks from his exertions, the streets narrowed and roads led off the main street past houses, bars, and open-fronted shops.

"This is VC territory," I pointed out. Off-limits.

O'Brien threw his head back and laughed. I laughed, too. The whole world had taken on a mellow glow by now.

"Are we going to let a few dinks keep our buddy from getting fucked?" O'Brien asked. "Besides, that's why they make us take our rifles to town. So we can fight off gooks in the whorehouses."

149

We cranked rounds into our M-14s and, laughing and giggling, felt ready for whatever came first—a fuck or a fight.

The sicylo stopped in front of a plain, two-story concrete house with wooden shutters closed over the windows. Light seeped out around the edges, although it was still daylight. No Marines were allowed in town after dark. Out front a sidewalk vendor had his pushcart stocked with everything from dried squid to ballpoint pens. Our driver bobbed his head.

"Numbah one boom-boom house," he announced. "Numbah one Hong Kong boom-boom girls."

Smitty wanted a condom from the sidewalk vendor. "You souvenir me one rubber?" he asked in mock pidgin English.

I looked at him. "You don't have any money?"

"You guys promised to get me laid. I figure a rubber's included."

"Jee-suz Kee-rist."

A short, fat mamasan showed us up a narrow stairway to the second floor, the entirety of which was one huge room partitioned off into small cubicles by brightly painted plaster board. The overhead lights were dim. We could hear pleasureable sounds coming from some of the cubicles.

The place was like a maze used in rat labs. Mamasan didn't get us lost. She led us to one of the enclosures which contained only a bare mattress on a double bed on top of which a naked young Vietnamese girl languidly sprawled. She looked at the three of us without curiosity. It was customary for GIs not to come alone. That way one could bed while the others kept watch, just in case.

Smitty leered and immediate began tearing off his khakis. The girl, who looked no older than sixteen, did not change expressions.

"Eager, ain't he?" O'Brien said.

I dragged the Arab, protesting, into the passageway outside the cubicle to give Smitty his privacy, although Smitty didn't seem to care one way or the other. "A stiff dick don't get embarrassed." There were a number of fist-sized holes in the plaster board, apparently left by drunken GIs. O'Brien bent down to peek through one.

"What are you doing?"

"Watching Smitty get laid. We paid for it, didn't we?"

I thought about it a moment, then shrugged and followed his example. O'Brien could be ruthlessly logical at times. I was just in time to catch Smitty standing huge at the foot of the bed naked except for his helmet liner, one boot, and a broad Missouri grin. He opened his foil pack and slipped on the rubber. He was ready for action.

Suddenly, the girl *had* an expression. It was terror. She bolted upright in bed, staring.

"No! No! Numbah *ten*."

Startled, Smitty's foolish grin withered. He looked down at himself.

"What the fuck's the matter with you, darling?"

"No! No!"

The girl pointed. Three sets of eyes followed the line of her finger. O'Brien began to snicker. Dangling obscenely off the end of Smitty's well-stretched rubber was a French tickler three inches long, looking like the waddles off a turkey gobbler. Smitty's grin came back.

"Ain't it purty?" he said, reaching for his darling.

She wanted none of that. She jumped out of bed.

"You bitch," Smitty said.

"Nice little ass," O'Brien noticed.

Smitty had put off getting laid as long as he intended to. The chase was on, around the room and over the bed, Smitty's turkey gobbler waddle whipping absurdly about, the little whore screaming for rescue. She tried to get out the door, but O'Brien blocked it. The giant American wearing his helmet, one boot, and French tickler, and the tiny boom-boom girl, keeping just out of reach of his clutches, made a half-dozen laps of the cubicle before the commotion attracted mamasan.

Mamasan panted up the stairs and charged through the maze like a full column of VC. O'Brien and I were laughing so hard that mamasan almost dodged past us before O'Brien latched onto her and shoved her back down the stairs. She kept her feet by running out of control all the way to the bottom before she collapsed in a pool of Vietnamese curses.

That brought papasan, who was as thin as mamasan was fat. Swinging his arms and hissing in imitation of Bruce Lee, he rushed us. I waited until he reached the top of the stairs before I planted a quick foot square in his chest. Pain shot through the punji wound. Papasan picked himself up from the bottom of the stairs and scurried into the street, yelling, *"MP! MP! MP!"*

Smitty was still in hot pursuit. O'Brien looked at me.

"The Marines do not have a word for retreat," he said, slurring his words.

"Fuck it. Invent one."

*"Di-di mao?"* he asked.

"How about—*Let's get the fuck out of Dodge?"*

"Speaking of fucking—" O'Brien jerked a thumb toward the commotion behind us.

An MP whistle shrilled in the street outside. The MPs were always good about warning us they were coming.

"Smitty ain't no rabbit," I said. "There ain't time."

"It'll break his heart."

"Better his heart than his head."

By the time we cornered the rampaging Missourian and grabbed his clothes and rifle, MPs were forging into the foyer downstairs. There was only one way to escape—through a window. We forgot we were on the second floor. Smitty threw open the window and looked down, then shrugged and went sailing into the air with one boot on and everything else in his arms. We heard him hit with a thud and a grunt.

The MPs were coming up the stairs. We had no choice. One after the other, we leaped out the window after Smitty, and one after the other we landed in an open "benjo" sewer that ran down the back alleys.

"Jee-suz Kee-rist, it's *shit.*"

By the time we got back to the airbase, Smitty had lost all his uniform in the insane race down back alleys except for one boot, his trousers, helmet liner, and M-14. The stench of the sewers preceded us by a hundred meters. The gate guards wrinkled their noses and motioned us through while keeping their distance.

Sergeant Shireman caught us sneaking into our bunkers. He couldn't have caught a more sheepish trio of Marines. He stopped and sized us up. Smitty still had the French tickler clutched in one hand. Then the sergeant shook his head and walked on by as though nothing had happened.

"Had a good time in town, I see," he said.

# Chapter 21

SURVIVAL DEPENDED UPON LUCK, or fate, or chance, or predestination. Whatever. It depended on that more than upon anything you did or did not do. You could be the most careful grunt in 'Nam, always doing the extra little things the DIs said would help keep you alive, like keeping your rifle oiled and cleaned, digging your hole deeper, staying awake on watch, and never taking unnecessary risks, playing it safe, and still some fruit jar filled with powder and nails would get you, or a fourteen-year-old gook with a bolt-action rifle, or a French mine.

"It ees like if your number comes up, she comes up," said Frenchy. "There ees nothing you can do about it. You take your number and hold onto it and hope the Man does not call it. And if He does call it, hope He called the wrong number by mistake."

"Bullshit," said Sergeant Shireman. "The Man calls my number, He'll wish He called the wrong number. He better call it good and loud 'cause this gyrene is going down kicking and screaming and sonofabitching."

About Sergeant Shireman, you knew it was true.

We crossed the river again and settled into the by-now familiar routine of patrols and sweeps and digging in around some village.

"Goddamnit, right back to the field," I complained. "You know what that means, don't you?"

O'Brien nodded. "It means we're going to get shot at again."

"No. It means we're going to have to dig more fucking holes."

Frenchy had a way of ending a conversation with a single sentence. "That ees not true, my friend," he said. "We have already dug them all."

The monsoons were not over yet. It still rained every day between short bouts with sunshine, and the mud caked on your boots until each foot felt like it had a LRDB—Little Round Dink Boat—attached to it. A war without mud was as unimaginable as drinking shit water without Kool-Aid.

"It's a master plan," O'Brien decided. "J. C. and The Boys up there cook you with the sun, drown you in rain, throw mud all over you, and torment you with little things like leeches and snakes and mosquitos and the screaming shits. That's to make life miserable. Then They put gooks down here to shoot at you. That's to make life interesting."

He shook his head.

"It don't make fucking sense, none of it," he said.

But then he shook his head again and said in that way he had, "Jee-suz Kee-rist," and it somehow didn't matter if it didn't make sense. That was just the way it was.

Every time that mysterious *someone* moved our pin, the mushrooms—kept in the dark and fed horse shit—got up and went somewhere else.

Amtracks in a long line left the road and followed the lead vehicles as it nosed and slid down a muddy embankment to a rice paddy. The squatty green amphibs filled with Marines belched smoke and ground gears, lurching and rattling through the water, until the leader bogged down and came to a protesting halt with its tracks spinning. That stopped all the other monsters. For all their roaring and belching, they could not get started again. Slinging mud and water, they slowly sank past their spinning tracks. The mighty, mechanized, modern U.S. Marine Corps had been stopped by a centuries-old rice paddy.

"End of the road, ladies." Sergeant Shireman stood on top of the lead track, grinning and motioning for the platoon to dismount into the water. "Drop your meat and hit your feet."

The stalled monsters gave birth to their progeny of Marines. After much shouting and splashing about, the company waded forward on line toward a bamboo tree line that harbored the village complex called An Trach. Our mission—search and destroy. Mostly it was search since daylight sweeps, even with the escalation of the war, rarely turned up anything worth destroying. The company's orders were to sweep through and dig in on the other side next to the Tuy Loan River. A Marine battalion would snap onto our flank later in the week to complete the newest extension of the enclave around Da Nang.

"I guess we ain't dug all the holes there are," I grumbled to Frenchy.

"We are digging zee same holes over and over again," Frenchy explained.

An ONTOS antitank vehicle accompanied the sweep. Instead of following the larger tracks into the rice paddy, it had circled around, staying on the dikes. It was growling and lurching along on a dike to my left as the Marines reached the first few hootches and entered the ville. I glanced away to catch something Leslie was saying. When I looked back around, the ONTOS had simply disappeared. No one I had ever met could express himself like O'Brien in so many ways using the same few syllables.

"Jee-suz Kee-rist."

He was pointing at the dike. In a second, the ONTOS crew came scrambling up out of the earth itself. Curious, I veered toward the dike to find the tank killer nosed down into the largest punji trap I had ever seen. The pit was at least seven feet deep and wide enough and long enough to swallow an entire ONTOS. Sharpened bamboo stakes three feet long pin-cushioned the bottom and sides of the hole. Any men stepping onto the concealed mat covering the pit would have dropped through to certain death.

By luck, fate, chance, what have you, the ONTOS had gone through instead of some of the Marines.

The bamboo fence lines in the village started splitting the company into platoons and the platoons into squads. It was Dum-Dum Duminski's turn to run point on squad. Neither he nor McNey had been blinded after all by the booby trap gate during Operation Starlight. They got out of the hospital and were sent back to the platoon. The only way out of Vietnam, McNey complained, was in a box.

Duminski's hand shot up suddenly and he froze. As always, McNey was right behind him. They were a pair. Duminski snapped a warning:

"Hold it. Stay back. I think I'm standing on something."

"What the fuck you talking about?" That was McNey.

"I'm standing on *something*. Get Bellot up here."

Bellot was already working his way forward.

"Don't come too close," Duminski said, whispering, as though the vibrations from his voice might be enough to spring whatever he was standing on. From all appearances, he was on solid ground, but balanced on a thin, invisible line. The squad eased cautiously forward.

"A mine?" someone asked.

The Pole's face popped sweat from every pore. This time he might not be as lucky as before. Some villagers stood back in the shade of their hootches and, expressionless, watched the drama unfolding.

"We'll get the engineers over," Bellot said, "Just don't move, goddamnit, don't move."

"It ain't a mine," Duminski whispered. "It's something else."

McNey's thin face stretched into angles a face was not supposed to have as he watched his buddy struggle against almost paralyzing fear.

157

"Dum-Dum . . . ? We'll get you out of this."

Eyes riveted on the Marine; beginning to act, he slowly attached his bayonet to his rifle. Then he began to probe around with it. The bayonet sank effortlessly into the ground.

He was standing in the center of a big punji trap like the one that claimed the ONTOS. For some reason, he had not dropped through. Any movement now—even that of his strictured breathing—might be sufficient to send him tumbling through to be impaled like a beetle on pins.

His lips barely moved. "Get me off it," he begged hoarsely, whispering.

"Just don't move. Don't move."

A chicken came clucking down the path toward us, heading mindlessly for Duminski. Duminski's eyes bugged. No one dared make any sudden movements for fear of startling him.

O'Brien was nearest the chicken. "Dum-Dum, I'm gonna kick that chicken's ass for you," he said, trying to make light of it to ease the tension.

It worked. "Get . . . body count," Dum-Dum croaked.

That gave O'Brien the chance to act. He waved his arms and shouted, veering the fowl from its original path. It fast-legged around the trapped Marine and, squawking, disappeared into the bamboo. The villagers watched, unmoving.

"Smitty. Roberts. Find out how big the pit is," Bellot ordered.

Duminski's pleading eyes followed as we carefully probed with our own bayonets to outline an area roughly four feet square around the living statue.

"Maybe I can jump to the side," Duminski suggested.

That was considered—and rejected.

"You might collapse it," advised Bellot.

"Do *something*," Duminski urged.

I was looking around. My eyes lit on a stand of bamboo, thick, strong, green stuff forty feet high.

"We can take a long pole," I pointed out, indicating the

bamboo, "with a man on each end and walk it to him. He can grab ahold in the center and we'll lift him off."

"Roberts, you're a fucking genius," Smitty said. "Read that in your Kipling?"

It worked. Once again, Duminski cheated death. He had tears in his eyes as he went around hugging everyone. Show over, the villagers melted away.

The trap had a stout bamboo rod stretched across the center of the hole underneath a camouflaged mat. The rod served as a fulcrum for a lid that rotated around it. Weight on either side of the pole flipped up the opposite side and dropped the rear side, dumping the victim onto the spikes below.

By chance, Duminski had stepped directly on the pivot pole itself.

"The Man," Frenchy said philosophically, "He called zee wrong number by mistake."

# Chapter 22

IF YOU LOOKED AT IT that way—that when your number came up, it came up no matter where you were, whether back on the block at home crossing a street in front of a Mack truck or here in Vietnam getting shot at by gooks— then you didn't have to worry about it anymore. If the Man picked the wrong number, He'd let you have the chance to show Him.

At least that was how Frenchy saw it.

It took Third Battalion two days to dig in on the high ground facing the river beyond An Trach. The river was wide at this point from the monsoons and ran a dirty, foam-flecked hemorrhage red. The land on our side of the river dropped off in a bluff to the water, while a lowland swamp fringed the opposite side. Beyond the swamp were more rice paddies and another village, part of the An Trach complex.

Snipers periodically slipped into the swamp and harassed us, safe from pursuit because of the river. The platoons set up sniper watches, but the VC managed nonetheless to sneak in, pop off a few rounds, and then get back out before the Marines poured withering fire down on them.

Otherwise, we labored like coolies digging holes and filling sandbags while transistor radios blared like at a picnic in a park.

. . . hang on, Sloopy . . . Sloopy, hang on-n-n-n . . .

McNey and some of the others were filling sandbags on the bank of the river and passing them up a red clay wall to the rest of the platoon when a sniper's shot cracked from across the river. A look of consternation appeared on McNey's mail clerk face and he dropped a filled sandbag.

"Shit!"

A neat round hole in the flesh of his bare left forearm began to ooze blood. McNey just stood there looking at it, surprise turning to ecstasy, while I emptied a full magazine at a black-clad figure across the river. The VC darted into the swamp and escaped. McNey wasn't even noticing. Heedless of his wound, he was starting to jump around on the river bank shouting with joy.

"I got my *third* Heart!" he yelled at Sergeant Shireman, who ran up to see what was going on. "Sarge, I'm going home. I got my *third*. I'm gettin' outa this shithole place."

That was one way of getting out of Vietnam other than in a box. Three Purple Hearts automatically sent you home if you wanted to go. We all envied McNey his gunshot wound.

"Zat ees *three* wrong numbers," Frenchy said.

"That was a *right* number," McNey corrected happily. "It's getting me out of Vietnam, ain't it? I'll say hello for you to the good ol' U.S. of A."

A battalion of the First Marines dug in on our flank across the river where the sniper'd come from. The battalion was so new in-country that the Marines' uniforms were still new and dark. VC liked to break newbys in right, attacking them and leaving the vets be; they attacked the First Marines the first night they were digging in. Some of us in the Third Battalion sat on the bluff on our side of the river and watched the fireworks, sometimes cheering like spectators at a football game. The fight continued for almost an hour, exchanging red and green tracers, before the night fell silent and only parachute flares continued to hiss upward to light the river and the swamp in front of the new battalion's lines.

The routine of day patrols and night patrols and sweeps continued out of An Trach as it had out of all the other places around which we had dug in. I was beginning to lose track of all the different names. I was, however, learning to have more respect for Frenchy's theory about when your number came up.

One afternoon on a platoon patrol we received fire from a small concrete shrine on the outskirts of An Trach. Lieutenant Rowe called for the 3.5 rocket launcher team rather than risk men to uproot the sniper. The team huffed up with its tube and looked across a wide rice paddy at the shrine set in a grove of palms, like a jewel in a mounting. The ammo bearer slipped a rocket into the back of the tube, got it ready, and slapped the gunner on the helmet as a signal to fire. The gun rested on the firer's left shoulder. He sighted carefully. I held my ears against the backblast.

Surprised Marines gawked as the rocket made a weird high climb to the right and exploded on the other side of the hamlet, sending water buffalo, kids, and chickens running.

The rocketeers looked stunned. "A dud," they explained.

They quickly reloaded and fired. The second missile streaked for the shrine, but then, at the last moment, climbed straight for the sun. Another dud.

"This has never happened before," the befuddled rocketeers said.

The third rocket ran out of energy and skipped across the rice paddy like a flat stone on water. It scooted up the small mud bank on the other side and struck the wall of the shrine with a dull thud, failing to go off. An entire platoon of Marines, too surprised to react, watched as the sniper vacated the temple like he had been goosed out of his hole.

"It wasn't his number," Frenchy theorized, laughing. "He had better kiss ol' Buddha's ass thank you tonight."

Even Sergeant Shireman was looking with new respect on Frenchy the Philosopher, until we learned that the rocket motors soaked up moisture when carried in the open on a packboard and thus behaved erratically.

"Frenchy, you're a shitbird," Sergeant Shireman said.

But from then on we left the rocket launcher in the rear with the flame thrower. The launchers set up on line to guard the base, for whatever value they were, while the flame throwers, which could not be used in Vietnam because of some kind of political agreement between the leaders, were utilized to burn out the contents of the outdoor shitters on the airbase perimeter.

Sergeant Shireman again looked at the merits of Frenchy's philosophy a few days later when the platoon cut through a tree line and entered a small clearing where we surprised two gooks leaning on their weapons talking. They were less than fifty meters away. Tommy Shands, who was running point, immediately popped point-blank at the gooks with his M-79 grenade launcher.

The grenade struck directly between the first VC's legs and exploded.

The explosion lifted the gook about two inches off the ground. He landed on his feet, obviously as astonished as the rest of us, and took off running after the other gook. That was the last we saw of them.

Frenchy swiped off his helmet and scratched his head.

"Do you suppose," he speculated, "that zee dinks and us are all working from zee same set of numbers?"

Sergeant Shireman merely looked at Frenchy, saying nothing.

# Chapter 23

IN HIS UNIT AID BAG, Doc Lindstrom was as apt to be carrying grenades and extra .45 ammo for his pistol as battle dressings. He was Navy—all corpsmen with the Marines were Navy—but Doc was as good a Marine as anyone in the platoon. If you got hit and needed Doc, you could count on looking up and seeing his long Ichabod Crane frame and thick horn-rimmed glasses rushing toward you, no matter how much shit was coming down. He could patch you up with one hand and fire his .45 with the other, then drag or carry you back home. Doc Lindstrom had guts. Navy or not, Doc Lindstrom was Marine.

There was only one thing wrong with the Doc. He couldn't see after dark. He may as well have been in the depths of a cave. It was Doc's night blindness that caused him to be left behind in the cane field with the sniper.

That was after An Trach. Our pin got moved and the mushrooms were yanked up again and sent to Le Son. It was a different experience for Marines who had come to expect nothing of the Vietnamese villagers except inscrutable stares, indifference, and occasional outright hostility. The inhabitants of Le Son were *friendly* in the real sense of the word. They showed us pictures of relatives wearing ARVN uniforms. The kids came out and wanted to play with us. We found no booby traps or trip wires or punji stakes or hidden VC tunnels, just the usual family bomb shelter dug in the floor of each hut.

Kept safe from the Viet Cong's excessive forced taxation, it was a prosperous village. The rice urns were full, with more rice drying in large flat baskets in the courtyards. Smiling people cooked over charcoal fires in their straw-topped hootches, while others worked tending rice in the fields.

For once, we thought we were going to get the clean end of the stick. Doc Lindstrom peered myopically about through his Coke bottles and happily began to treat a kid with large runny sores.

The battalion swept peacefully through Le Son and dug in on perimeter. It seemed we had dug enough holes to sink the entire peninsula into the South China Sea.

A sugar cane field tall enough and thick enough to have concealed a full company of VC blocked our view to the front. Someone suggested calling in a fire mission to level the cane field, but Phil Leslie nipped that suggestion with a little chant we had made up to the tune of "Bless 'em All":

We asked for the arty to support us at Cam Ne;
The Arty appeared on the scene.
They knocked out two monkeys, five oxen, four chickens,
And seven platoons of gyrenes.

We should have known friendly smiles and happy natives were too good to last. It was not long after the companies and platoons got settled in than sniping began from the cane field. It seemed obligatory for the VC to provide at least one sniper for each platoon of Marines; sometimes we thought the same one followed us from place to place. It was a kind of job security. As long as the sniper did not do any damage, shooting just enough to satisfy his superiors, he was relatively safe. It was only the ambitious ones who were in danger of short-lived careers.

The sniper in the cane field was ambitious. And punctual. He showed up every evening around dark and popped off a round about once an hour until 3:00 A.M., at which time he packed up his tools and went home to get ready for a hard day's work in his rice field.

He punctured Smitty's packboard and kept Lieutenant Rowe lying flat in his hole for an hour. It wasn't until he let off a round at Sergeant Shireman when Sergeant Shireman was trying to answer a call of nature in the woods, thereby interrupting the platoon hero at his daily toilette, that we had our fill of him.

"Dirty little shitbird!" Sergeant Shireman raged, stomping down the line in open view buttoning his pants, as though double-dog daring the sniper to try it again. "That little cocksucking asswipe has got to go."

That night Second Platoon went out on patrol. Corporal Bellot drew a crude map in the dirt for the squad.

"Here's the scoop. We're going to sweep the cane field for the sniper as soon as he gets here, then meet the other two squads here." He jabbed a stick. "Then the platoon'll head here to see what that light is that's burning in the village every night."

What made it strange was that no one ordinarily turned on a light in the war zone. It was about a kilometer away.

"I'll take point," Bellot said. He already had his .45 and grenade ready. "Yates, you follow me, then Smitty, Leslie, Renninger, Michaud, Roberts, Raglund, O'Brien. Ekstein's team brings up the rear. Doc Lindstrom is coming with us, so somebody grab ahold of him and be his seeing-eye dog."

The patrol heated up camouflage sticks with Zippos and mixed the paints with insect repellent to rub into our skin. Faces blackened, we taped down anything loose that would rattle. Then we formed up at dusk and moved out to the edge of the cane field to wait for the sniper to come.

We didn't wait long. A gunshot echoed from the far edge

of the field. That was the signal for the platoon, on line, to go crashing into the cane with all the stealth and silence of a herd of water buffalo. You simply cannot move silently through sugar cane.

I struggled forward, isolated by the cane, until I broke free on the other side into a clearing briefly lit by a moon playing coy with rain clouds. A figure sat hunched on a grave mound at the end of the clearing. The figure stirred and said, "Yates?"

I recognized O'Brien's voice and walked toward him. The clouds obscured the moon and plunged the clearing into greater darkness.

"Yates?"

I kept walking until I heard the telltale *click* of an M-14 being eased off SAFE. The moon came out and illuminated O'Brien. He was pointing his rifle at my chest.

"O'B?" I said quickly.

"Jee-suz Kee-rist, Roberts. I thought you was the sniper. Why didn't you answer me?"

" 'Cause you was talking to Yates, not me."

O'Brien sounded peeved. "I just saved your fucking life, you skinny shit."

"How do you figure that?"

" 'Cause I didn't squeeze the trigger. I almost greased your ass."

The squad straggled in and reorganized and moved to a thorned bamboo fence to link up with the rest of the platoon. The sniper had escaped. After a break, I felt Frenchy tug on my sleeve. We were getting ready to move out in the direction of the strange light in the village. Doc Lindstrom was sitting on the side of a ditch staring blindly into the blackness in front.

The platoon wended its way through rice paddies and along a dike until, an hour later, Lieutenant Rowe called a halt in an old cemetery and asked for the squad leaders up. Bellot returned shortly.

"First and Third's gonna set up a blocking force with Sergeant Shireman and the lieutenant just to the west of here on a trail coming out of the village," he reported. "We're going to circle around the village and come in on the opposite side and see what we can flush out to them."

Everywhere you went you ended up wading waist-deep in rice paddies. We slogged across, climbed out of water, and trailed through a stand of dense jungle. No wonder my wound wouldn't heal.

We were entering the trees and bamboo surrounding the hamlet when a dark figure broke momentarily into moonlight, scurrying away at our approach. The moon hid again immediately, but we heard the soft thudding of running feet. We ran after the VC.

"O'Brien, Roberts, Frenchy—go to the left!" Bellot ordered.

Frenchy and O'Brien disappeared into the bushes. Trotting, favoring my sore leg, I skirted a thin stand of bamboo until I came to an opening. I slipped through the opening and paused to listen. I could hear Frenchy and O'Brien, but I could see nothing. It was almost total blackness.

I felt my way forward, vaguely making out a fringe of trees to my right and what I thought might be a hootch directly ahead.

Abruptly, a rifle opened up on automatic. I hit the ground instinctively just as tracers buzzed into the wall of a trench ahead of me. Tracers sizzling in the mud cast an eerie reddish glow that outlined O'Brien's form. He was sending lead streaming down a trench and through the entrance to a tunnel where the VC had escaped, secure in the knowledge that we would not follow him there.

The rest of the squad came running. O'Brien explained and pointed out the tunnel.

"That gook's gone out the other end by now," Bellot decided. "Let's get a move on."

The squad swept forward on line.

"This place stinks of ambush," Bellot whispered. "That light's in a hootch. See it? Roberts, toss in a trip flare to light it up. If it's VC, I'll follow with a grenade and Roberts and I'll zap anybody that runs out. O'Brien, Frenchy, take the right flank. Duminski and Ekstein—the left.''

It would take a stupid VC to still be in the hootch with the light on after all the commotion. Stupid—or cunning enough to set a trap for us.

Again I lost sight of the others and of the hootch with the light on. I stumbled my way through another thick bamboo fence and emerged, almost bumping into Bellot. The fence had delayed our advance.

Bellot had his grenade in hand. I was sure the pin was pulled. Ahead of us lay a single hootch with a square outline, probably a concrete one. Yellow light glowed pale through a window and through an open door at one end. I eased the pin from my flare, to be ready.

We crept forward side by side. My little furry creature was starting to knead its claws.

It almost leaped out my throat when muzzle flashes accompanied by loud staccato chatter erupted directly in my face—for the second time within the last few minutes.

I AIN'T GETTING OUT ALIVE!

I hit the dirt—and dropped the flare. Trip flares go off instantaneously with a brilliant hot light. This one flamed almost underneath my helmet, stinging my face and blinding me. I rolled desperately to the left to get away from it and from the ambush I was sure we had walked into.

And fell screaming into space.

I landed in a crumple at the bottom of a five-foot-deep dry well. I lay there a moment, stunned and disoriented. As vision returned, I saw bright light above. I heard more shooting. Then Bellot was yelling.

"O'Brien, what the hell is going on?"

"It's a goddamned VC!" O'Brien shouted. "A goddamned gook with a weapon and some old lady ran out of the hootch when me and Frenchy come up."

"Fuck they did," Bellot yelled angrily. "You scared the shit out of us."

"They were laying for you," O'Brien said smugly, "but

me and Frenchy surprised their yellow asses, didn't we, Frenchy?"

"You missed them," came Frenchy's unexcited response.

Unnerved, half-blinded, and feeling sorely put upon, I crawled out of the well. Frenchy sniggered; he grinned a lot, but he never really laughed. That was the nearest to it I ever heard.

"Roberts, how fast you can dig zee hole," he exclaimed. "And so deep, too."

I limped up to where O'Brien was busy exploring the inside of the hut. There was nothing left behind to show why the kerosene lamp was burning in the middle of a cleared table. O'Brien scratched his head.

"I just saved your goddamned life," I said. It was my turn to be peeved.

"Yeah? How?"

" 'Cause I didn't throw a grenade at you when you started shooting, you crazy Arab fuck."

O'Brien's skin glowed swarthy in the dim light. "I guess that makes us even," he said. "I wonder why those dumb gooks had this light on."

The two most dangerous grunts in Vietnam, I thought dourly, were Roland O'Brien and Craig Roberts—dangerous to each other.

It was not until after we uneventfully completed the sweep and linked up with the rest of the platoon that Sergeant Shireman strode among us looking.

"Where's Doc?" he asked. "Have you shitbirds lost Doc?"

The question swept through the platoon.

"Who was supposed to be watching him?" someone asked.

That sent Sergeant Shireman into a rage. "I don't give a goddamned flying fuck *who* was supposed to be watching him. You're all supposed to be watching him. If you puke birds lost Doc, I'll personally make you eat your own balls. Now, where is he?"

After some hurried discussion, it was generally agreed

that the last time anyone saw Doc was at the ditch by the cane field. There was a long moment of silence as the realization sank in. It required little imagination to know what the VC did to Marines they caught alone. None of us was ever likely to forget the wiremen found hanging in the tree.

Bellot's voice sounded oddly strained. "Roberts, Yates—go back to the ditch and find him."

Thoughts of Doc Lindstrom strung up by his heels put wings on our feet. The poor blind sonofabitch couldn't have seen the VC even if they walked right up and pissed on him. He had to cling to someone's pack straps whenever he went on night patrol.

Yates and I threw aside all caution as we raced along the dike that bordered the cane field. My leg didn't even bother me.

We easily found the clearing and crossed it to the thorned bamboo fenceline. Yates stumbled into the ditch. We paused to listen.

Nothing.

We crept one behind the other along the bottom of the ditch, expecting the worse. Yates grabbed my shoulder. We both stopped to stare at a silent, still form blocking our path. It looked propped up and unlifelike.

*Doc? No!*

The VC had a habit of booby-trapping our KIAs or using them as ambush decoys. Yates indicated by sign language that he would circle to the right to cover me. He moved off quietly while I cautiously approached the form in the ditch. I knew I must, but I dreaded seeing what mischief the sniper and his buddies had done to Doc.

I squatted and looked around before I reached out to touch Doc, lightly, in case his body had been booby-trapped.

Doc gave an unexpected start of surprise. My hand shot back like I had touched fire.

"Doc . . . Doc, are you all right?"

Doc's head lolled to find the direction of my voice.

"Yeah, sure," he whispered. He hadn't budged since we

171

left him. "We've been here a long time," he said. "Is it time to move out yet?"

Pete Yates and I exchanged looks of relief. Doc Lindstrom hadn't even known we were gone.

"Yeah, Doc," I said, gently taking his sleeve. "It's time to move out."

# Chapter 24

Most of the time, a bayonet is just so much dead weight, an anachronism in an era of massive firepower. Le Son was possibly the scene of the first, and last, bayonet charge in the Vietnam War. It seemed like a good idea at the time.

Second Platoon came under stiff automatic weapons fire while patrolling a network grid of narrow dikes separating rice paddies. There was a clatter of fire from a tree line, accompanied by bullet geysers dancing down the dike toward the lead element like a hot breath across the surface of a lake. With a howl of surprise, Marines tumbled behind the dike for cover.

Every time we stuck up our heads to return fire, the gooks opened up from the tree line about three hundred meters away. Sergeant Shireman cursed an uninterrupted streak of profanity with a talent that had become the envy of the entire battalion. Lieutenant Rowe, attempting to raise fire support on the PRC-10 radio, finally gave up in frustration and cast the radio handset on the ground.

"Goddamned radio is out again."

He rarely cursed.

Doc Lindstrom crawled up and down the line checking for casualties. Pete Yates thrust his rifle over the lip of the dike and sprayed bullets in the general direction of the tree line while keeping his head down. He grinned a lazy Ozark grin at Smitty, who, thinking it a good idea, followed suit. About half the platoon opened blind fire at the enemy in the same way.

"Goddamn!" Sergeant Shireman yelled. "Who taught you pukes to shoot?"

"You did," somebody yelled back.

"Goddamn!" said Sergeant Shireman.

It was broad daylight, sun shining, on an operation that should have been a milk run, another stroll in the sun—and the goddamed gooks had pinned us down. We could not withdraw and we could not move forward. Exposure of so much as the top of a helmet invited a withering hail of lead from the jungle.

Lieutenant Rowe, normally calm and unassuming under fire, jammed a fresh clip into the butt of his .45 pistol and looked around, scowling his displeasure.

"What do they think we are—the fucking Army?" he yelled.

He emptied his pistol shooting over the top of the dike, although the enemy lay well out of range of his .45. That did not seem to improve his temperament. He never could stand to see his men placed on the defensive by a few little raggedy-ass yellow men in black pajamas. He rolled over on his back and glared at the sun. The muscles in his jaws twitched. Somebody down the dike revealed a target and the gooks chewed up the terrain.

Enough was enough. The lieutenant sprang to his knees and waved his pistol.

"That's *it*, goddamnit!" he shouted in a manner more characteristic of Sergeant Shireman than of Lieutenant Rowe. Marines looked his way in uncertain surprise.

*"Fix bayonets!"*

No one questioned the order. For too long booby traps, mines, and snipers had picked us off one by one in a war that seldom had a definable objective or an enemy we could close with and kill. It was about time *something* was done about it. I felt the adrenaline start to pump as the click of bayonet lugs up and down the line locked long knives into place. Naturally, Sergeant Shireman was the first to stand up. The man was grinning. He ignored the fresh bursts of enemy fire.

"This," he shouted, "is *my* kind of war."

Maybe not at any other moment, but at *that* moment it was also *our* kind of war. The dirty little slant-eyed, shithead gooks had it coming. We were the U.S. by-God Marines, the finest fighting men in the world. Maybe it was a little late, but we would still have the hot beach landing denied us. No more "Co' Cola, Joe?"

All up and down the line, grunts who, for too long, had been baffled by ghosts who rarely seemed to die, stood up with sharpened bayonets gleaming in the midday sun. The gooks must have been temporarily nonplussed at the sight, for their firing almost stopped. Lieutenant Rowe stood up and eyed his eager men with grim satisfaction.

"Ready!" he bugled. "Let's go. . . . *Charge !!* Go! Go! Go!"

A rebel yell, clear and piercing, announced the start of the charge. It was followed by a savage chorus from lusty young American throats. The platoon swarmed over the top of the dike in a scene reminiscent of trench warfare in WWI and stormed the jungle, screaming and war-crying and shooting from the hip. It was primitive, it was basic, it was foolhardy, but it was satisfying.

The yodeling, screaming, raging, ragged line of Marines assaulted across the open rice paddies like wild elephants. Panicky enemy fire went wild. Not a bullet touched a Marine. We burst into the tree line shouting and thrusting madly about with our bayonets.

Frenchy stopped first and stood in the damp shadows, catching his breath and looking dully about, as though

175

awakening from a trance. Then Smitty stopped. And O'Brien. And Duminski. And Raglund who, on the bridges, was unsure of what a *real* firefight was like.

Lieutenant Rowe's eyes came back into focus. He gave out a loud, tired sigh and went over and sat down on a tree root and held his head in his hands. Sergeant Shireman watched him; he dabbed at sweat on his face with a green bandanna tied loosely around his neck.

"Cowardly little pukes," he grumbled.

The VC had melted away again, leaving nothing behind for us to close with except the dark long lines of the shadows of bamboo.

# Chapter 25

OUR FIRST SNIPER in the sugar cane at Le Son was replaced by another. At least his rifle was replaced. One night a single shot boomed from the village that lay on the other side of the cane field and rice paddies from us. The shot did not snap or crack or pop—it *boomed*.

Although the village was a kilometer's distance from our lines, the bullet plunged through like a small rocket, toppling to the ground a bamboo stalk fifty feet tall and five inches in diameter. I heard O'Brien's astounded voice bay in the darkness.

"Jee-suz Kee-rist."

With that first introduction, the sniper with the cannon became the platoon's nemesis. Although at the range he was shooting, using the distant village as cover, he had to have been firing at random rather than picking his targets. Nevertheless, the sound of the heavy chunks of lead toppling bamboo around our ears and clawing whole chunks out of trees became unnerving enough to strike dread and outright terror into the hearts of Marines of the Second Platoon as soon as the sun started to set.

Patrols into the hamlet failed either to dislodge or discourage him. As soon as the Marines passed through, he was back in business harvesting bamboo around our ears. If he ever hit anyone, you could send the pieces home in a C-rat can.

Corporal Bellot gathered the squad. "We're going on ambush patrol tonight."

Leslie sighed. "We've been three times this week. Let me guess. The boom-boom sniper again?"

"The skipper wants him zapped."

Point was rotated among the members of the squad to equalize the risks. It was my turn. I led us into the rice paddies. It could get darker deeper and faster in Vietnam than anywhere else in the world. I took my time, stopping to listen and feel for trip wires and punji stakes. The weeping sore on my leg kept me aware of what sharpened bamboo poisoned with human excrement could do.

An hour later, having skirted the noisy cane field, the squad emerged from the paddies and used the dike trails to advance on the ville. It was a clear night, but there was no moon yet. Starlight was just sufficient to distinguish land from sky.

Shortly, I encountered a short bamboo fence just beyond a small Buddhist cemetery cratered with the typical round graves that had settled in on the dearly departed. Grave markers stood out like black ink scroll against the lighter sky. The gate to the village hung open and unguarded, as though in invitation. Halting the squad for a listening break, I heard the tinkling strains of music and the laughter and voices of young men and women. Lights muffled by blankets and thick curtains shone subdued from several hootches.

It had to be VC. There were no young civilians remaining in the hamlets, and ARVN would not have ventured out like this into the Viet Cong night. Bellot slipped up beside me.

"Sounds like a party," I whispered directly into the squad leader's ear, moving my lips while barely making the sounds.

Bellot sized up the situation, then whispered back the same way. "Hate to be a party crasher," he said, "but why don't we give 'em a little reception of our own when the party breaks up?"

"Why wait? The punch'll be all gone."

I felt Bellot grin as he patted his rifle. "We'll bring our own punch."

"How about the sniper?"

"He's probably drunk and passed out by now."

The squad set up in a classic U-shaped ambush formation focused on the open gate and the trail that ran through it to the village. The thing about Vietnamese hamlets was that the bamboo thorn fences forced everyone coming and going to use one of the several gates. Since our big-gun sniper did his work on this side of the village, he probably used this gate. If our luck held good, maybe we could catch him when the party broke up. So far, he hadn't been out to shoot at the Marine lines.

We waited, lying in the grave depressions, feeling and nursing the excitement of the hunt. I experienced an instant of déjà vu, then realized that this was almost a replay of the village ambush I had organized the night when the ARVN Rangers boogied out on me. There was one big difference this time though. Like my recruiter had said: ". . . your buddies won't bug out on you."

The party in the village grew louder before it started to break up. Near midnight, two shadows separated themselves from one of the hootches and walked toward the gate, again almost exactly a replay of that night with the Rangers. But, then, with this kind of war, you could experience all kinds of déjà vu since the war was nothing but a series of replays day and night after day and night.

"S.O.S.," the Marines said. "Same old shit."

The Vietnamese were smoking. The glow tips arced around their heads and I could smell the strong tobacco they used—another reason for suspecting they were VC, since the ARVN smoked American cigarettes whenever they could get them. The men ambled unsuspectingly through the gate and stopped to smoke and talk almost directly in the center of our ambush kill zone. One of them was leaning on a long walking stick.

How accommodating, I thought. The only thing that could have made it better was for them to have brought more VC with them—make this a real killing.

I held my breath with the tension, waiting on Bellot to initiate the ambush with a grenade.

I wondered why he was hesitating. You didn't have to see a weapon to know these two were the enemy. The starlight was bright enough to reveal that one wore a khaki uniform, which I took to be an NVA officer's, while the other was dressed in familiar basic black.

As I watched, the man in black smoked his cigarette and then, still jabbering, tossed it aside. He was the one with the walking stick taller than he was. He leveled it across the horizon before, surprised, I recognized it for what it was.

The biggest rifle I had ever beheld.

What incredible luck. Our big-gun sniper had stumbled into our grasp and *his* number was coming up, no mistake.

He squatted down on the trail with that giant's weapon and worked the bolt with a solid *ka-chunk!* Khaki Uniform pointed across the rice paddies toward the tree line that marked the Marine positions. Black Pajamas took aim.

When he fired, it sounded like a cannon. Flame gushed four feet from the muzzle. The recoil knocked the gunman flat on his ass. Khaki Uniform threw back his head and laughed. They were having great sport at it.

The sport did not last. Black Pajamas was still on his ass and Khaki Uniform was guffawing loudly when Bellot's grenade arced gracefully across the sky and landed between the enemy with a heavy thud. The laughter froze in Khaki Uniform's throat an instant before the grenade exploded in a flash of flame and the ambushers unleashed the fury of automatic weapons.

The explosion hurled the bodies out from the center, but lead ripped through the air before the chunks of meat and cloth hit the ground. Burst after burst continued, chewing up every inch of the kill zone. It was overkill, but *these* gooks were not going to jump up and run off *this time*.

Bellot had some difficulty regaining control. *"Cease fire! Cease fire!"*

Firing rattled to silence. *"Search 'em,"* Bellot yelled, leading the way for the search team.

Normally, the villagers hid in their bomb shelters when firing started and kept still and quiet. This time, however, lights went out in the village and there was a sudden buzz of activity. People were darting everywhere. *Lots* of people. It was like we had taken a long stick and poked it into a nest of hornets. What the hell kind of party had we crashed?

As usual, O'Brien had the best expression for it: "Jee-suz Kee-rist."

In the Marines, there might not be a word for retreat or retrograde, but there was nothing saying in which direction you had to attack, nor how fast you should attack in that direction. When a horde of men came swarming out of the village toward us, rifles and machine guns blazing, the squad chose to attack in the direction of our own lines. After loosing a few bursts to slow down the horde of gooks, we attacked at a very rapid pace.

We went running away from the hamlet and along a dike, strung out and panting like long distance runners. That was another time when I never gave thought to my leg. We kept running even after the enemy, with a few last shots, called off the chase.

It was a bedraggled and winded grunt patrol that finally found its way back to Third Battalion's perimeter.

"What the fuck did you run into out there?" Sergeant Shireman wanted to know. "It sounded like you took on the entire NVA. Did you win?"

Bellot explained and showed him and Lieutenant Rowe our booty, consisting of a leather pistol belt containing a map case and the rank insignia off Khaki Uniform's shirt collar. It was an insignia we had never seen before. The belt was shredded and bloody.

Although the heavy rifle had been left behind in our haste

to depart, Bellot had had the foresight to pick up the expended cartridge casing and take it with him. It was identified as a Russian antitank round of approximately fifty caliber. No wonder the recoil knocked the gook on his ass.

A few days passed before we learned who we had encountered at the ambush. Bellot returned from a meeting at the platoon CP and assembled the squad.

"That stuff we took from the dinks got a reading back from S-2," he said. "S-2 said they had heard of Chinese advisers being with the VC, but this was the first hard evidence of it. The gook in the khakis was a goddamned Red Chinese officer."

A hush descended upon the squad. Back at Pendleton, the vets from the Korean War were always talking about how the war was won until the Chicoms started sending their hordes across the border. Was the same thing about to happen here?

"That ain't all," Bellot continued. "There were some papers in the pouch assigning the chink as a military technician to the North Vietnamese Army. The sniper wasn't wearing black pajamas; he had on a dark blue uniform. The VC weren't chasing us. That was the North-fucking-Vietnamese Army."

We were living in interesting times. Sergeant Shireman was going to get his Pork Chop Hill yet.

# Chapter 26

SOMETIMES ON PATROL we encountered water buffalo killed by artillery or caught in a crossfire. Occasionally we ran across in the jungle a Vietnamese whom some Marine patrol had killed and could not find. The stench of corpses too long baked by the sun and made soggy by the rain was thick and cloying, the odor of death and rot.

My leg had that kind of stench to it. It was October when I stepped on the punji stake and now it was January and I could not walk without hobbling. Doc Lindstrom treated the wound and did everything he could, but a dark streak appeared and ran inflamed up the calf of my leg to the knee. I remembered reading about gangrene in the Civil War.

Doctors did not go to the field with the troops. It was at the Battalion Aid Station (BAS), three echelons up past the platoon and company Navy corpsmen, that you first found real doctors. Doc Lindstrom kept sending me to the company chief corpsman named Swan with requests that I be Medevac'd back to Da Nang to see a doctor, but Swan resisted. Unlike Doc Lindstrom, who, if we were on the bunker line, was out there in a bunker with us and who, if it rained, got wet with us, Doc Swan would not leave his tent headquarters without a direct order. I found him laid out in his tent on a cot reading a book.

"My leg keeps getting worse," I advised him. "Doc Lindstrom thinks I ought to go back to BAS to see a doctor."

Swan gave a long-suffering sigh in a way that reminded me of Tee Wee Van and sat up. "I'll be the judge of that," he said.

I unwrapped the battle dressing for him. He took a quick look.

"All we can do is keep putting antibiotic ointment on it," he decided, with an air of dismissal as he picked up his book and thumbed to find his page. "You know how long it takes for something to heal out here."

I pointed at the streaks running up my leg from the eroded crater of the wound. "That looks like gangrene to me."

He made a face that said he did not have time or patience for amateur medics and remained intractable. "I can't authorize you to go to BAS. They'll just send you back. You're still able to walk and stand watch."

"What do you have to do to see a doctor?" I demanded. "Get carried in unconscious on a stretcher with a sucking chest wound?"

Swan had already returned to his book and his cot. "Roberts, quit malingering," he said, and turned a page.

I got up and hobbled out of the tent before I rammed a hypodermic up his ass. Not knowing where else to turn but determined that something be done, I limped to the company gunnery sergeant's tent. Bureaucracy is just as entrenched in combat rear lines as it is in the peacetime military at home. A "combat clerk" pounding two-fingered on a typewriter glanced up impatiently.

"What do you need?"

"I need to see the gunny."

"What do you need the gunny for?"

"That's between me and the gunny."

"Well, you can't see the gunny unless you get by me first."

That was the final straw. The jerk was a PFC clerk; I was a lance corporal, a *combat* lance corporal. I threw myself across the desk and nearly yanked the wimp out of his chair by the front of his shirt.

"PFC," I said, grinding out the words, "you will tell the gunny that Lance Corporal Roberts is here to see him—unless you want to be sitting in that chair with an M-14 up your ass, bayonet attached."

Before things went further, the gunny heard it and stepped out from behind a canvas curtain stretched across the back part of the tent.

"What do you need, Roberts?"

That initiated a process that propelled me to the Naval Support Activity near Marble Mountain, a real hospital in Quonset huts, the one we had watched from the bridges being attacked and burned. I saw women with round eyes—nurses—for the first time since arriving in Vietnam.

> We asked for the nurses to come to Da Nang.
> The nurses, they got here with ease,
> Their ass on the table, each bearing the label,
> "Reserved for the officers, please."

An ambulance took me to the hospital. When it stopped, I grabbed my rifle and struggled out.

"Hey, we're supposed to take you in on a stretcher."

"I walked into Vietnam; I'll walk out."

As I limped into the hospital, dirty and faded and perpetually tired, I glimpsed through a window another harried-looking blond grunt also entering the hospital. Lines had eaten deeply around the grunt's mouth and eroded the forehead. He looked to have had at least thirty years of a hard life.

With a start, I realized I wasn't looking through a window. I was looking into a *mirror*. I was down to 123 pounds.

"I've never seen anything like this before," exclaimed the

185

first doctor over my wound. "I just got here a few weeks ago. I want someone else to have a look."

Two or three doctors had a look. They took pictures and exclaimed and pushed and probed while, growing increasingly uneasy, I sat on an examining table with the object of so much attention stretched out in front and my combat gear on a table within reach.

"Punji stake, huh?" the doctors kept asking wonderingly.

The doctors went into a huddle. I tried to hear what they were saying. I knew it was bad news when they kept coming back for second and third looks. Finally, one broke with a professional expression on his face.

"I think we can save the knee joint," he said. "We'll try to leave a few inches of leg below the knee for prothesis."

He couldn't be talking to *me*. He was talking to the thin and aging man I had seen through the window that was not a window. For a long minute I was too stupefied to respond. It was like I was already dead. At nineteen years old, you can't face right away the prospect of losing part of your body. I could see Rita staring at me where I ended below the knee when I got back home.

"The knee?"

"Yes. I think we can save it."

"Save it?"

"You can have an artificial leg—it'll work almost as well as this one."

I looked up at him. It had taken that long for the message to sink in.

"No," I said.

"No? We don't have a choice."

Rita was not going to see a one-legged man tottering off an airplane. The doctors were looking at me.

"We always have a choice," I said.

Before the doctors could react, before I even realized fully what I was doing, my eyes fell on the grenades attached to my combat belt. I snatched one of them and hooked my thumb into the ring, thrusting it out toward the doctors at arm's length. It was the act of a desperate man. The doctors involuntarily stepped back, their eyes bulging.

"I am not going home with one leg," I vowed. "I either walk home, or I don't go home at all."

I was deadly serious, at least for that moment. It was that moment that counted.

"Go get the captain," one doctor whispered to another who, nearest the door, slipped out. A silent standoff continued until he returned with a Navy captain.

The captain was short with gray hair. We looked at each other. I turned to point the grenade at him. I felt tears in my eyes and my hands were trembling.

"He's gone crazy, sir," one of the doctors whispered, edging toward the door. "He has a grenade and has threatened to blow himself up unless we can save his leg."

The captain remained unexcited. "I can see he has a grenade," he said.

"We can't save his leg, sir. It's too far gone."

The captain stepped forward. "Put that thing down, son."

"Not until you promise not to cut off my leg."

I meant it. The captain gestured. "Mind if I have a look?"

I felt hope, just a little seep of it deep inside next to where the furry creature was beginning to stir.

"I'll jerk the pin if you try anything," I warned.

"I just want to look."

He poked and probed and sniffed and pressed while I held the grenade and my ground. In the Marines, there was no word for retreat.

At last he looked up with a smile. I felt hope start to trickle.

"You aren't going to lose anything, son," he decided. "These new people don't know anything about tropical medicine. That's why they send us old salts over here."

Later, I learned the captain had practiced his medicine as a young doctor in the Pacific during World War II.

"I want three injections of antibiotics a day—streptomycin, terramycin, and penicillin. I want the wound packed with Variadase jelly three times *daily* until the infection is arrested. After that, pack it with granulated sugar four times a day and change the dressing. We'll do a graft when the muscle regranulates. Got it?"

"Aye, aye, sir," the befuddled doctors chorused.

The captain turned a sympathetic smile on me. Did I dare hope? Was this just a ploy leading to my sedation and the ultimate loss of my leg anyhow?

"Now, son, would you mind letting us take care of your weapons for you while you're here? You won't need them, I promise you."

He could have had me courtmartialed.

"Sir, you're not bullshitting me?"

The smile turned a little sad. "Son, you'll be back humping the bush with your unit in no time."

# Chapter 27

I HAD CLEAN SHEETS, *real* sheets, and hot chow three times a day. Round-eyed nurses fussed over me, and stars like Robert Mitchum and Ann-Margaret and Johnny Rivers came to the Quonset wards—"Where you from? Keep up the good work"—while other stars like Jane Fonda, we learned to our dismay, were busy protesting the war and visiting Hanoi. I thought surely the gangrene had spread and killed me and, as the old saying went, I had gone to Heaven 'cause, Lord, I'd spent my time in hell in Vietnam.

But, then, after a while, the boredom set in, even worse than on the bridges watch. As the wound healed and I started to gain weight I began to miss O'Brien and Frenchy and the others and to wonder how they were faring. I hoped their pin on the map stayed green and lucky.

One afternoon O'Brien and Yates came grinning into the Quonset ward gripping their soft covers and appearing as bashful and diffident in the strange, ordered atmosphere of the hospital as boys playing hooky to go to a strip show.

They told me Mike Company was seeing action on Operation Sparrow Hawk as a ready reaction force.

"We rescued a bunch of Green Beenies from a Special Forces camp in A Shau," O'Brien said. "Jee-suz Kee-rist, Roberts. The Berets had ARVN strikers with them. So many ARVNs were hanging on the skids that we couldn't lift off. The ARVN officers finally started shooting their own men to get 'em off the skids so the choppers could get the hell out of there. Roberts, you wouldn't have believed it."

"Who all went in there?" I asked.

"First and Second Platoons," Yates said.

O'Brien grinned. "That was enough. There was only *one* regiment of NVA—and we had Sergeant Shireman."

I told them the story of how I managed to save my leg.

"Pukes," O'Brien said, losing his grin. "The doctors they send over here think we're meat for them to practice on until they can go back home and make real bucks."

"I ain't going home without all my pieces in working order," I still maintained.

Yates shook his head. "Wertz lost his foot, but he went home. He won't play football no more though."

O'Brien gave the matter some study. Around us in the ward were several Marines who had lost legs or arms or eyes. I wondered how many had been unnecessary losses due to the fact that the wounded men hadn't thought to take measures to prevent it. I shuddered at how near I came to being one of them.

"Going home's what's important," O'Brien said presently. "It's better to go home with some of your pieces left over here than not to go home at all."

My eyes darted around the ward. "Not for me it ain't," I declared.


Healing was a long and restless process. You could only read so much Kipling.

A corpsman named Jones and I had become friends by way of his changing my dressings. Knowing how bored I was, he stopped by my rack on his way through the ward.

He flashed a conspiratorial grin I knew to be the signal for some diversion or another he was always planning. He confirmed it.

"Wanna have some fun tonight?"

He glanced around with the slyness of a fox about to break into a hen house.

"Just be ready to go about midnight," he said. "We have a 'boot' to break in."

After lights out, I lay awake in the darkness hearing the sick and wounded groaning and crying out in their sleep. Soon, a shadow slipped into the ward. It was Jones. He handed me my crutches.

"We're going to the morgue," he whispered, hushing further inquiries. "Wait'll you see this pogue."

I crutched behind him across tarmac to a large Quonset near the helipad where American KIAs were kept temporarily for identification, sorting, and eventual shipping to Stateside. Three other corpsmen met us crouched outside underneath the square light of a window. Suppressing giggles, they motioned us to be quiet.

A morbid sense of humor was a decided asset in combat, but I still felt uncomfortable spying through the window. A young Navy corpsman as tall and thin as a pencil mark sat behind a desk with his feet propped up reading a book. Stateside rock 'n' roll issued from a radio at his elbow. He yawned, removed his glasses to rub his eyes, gazed myopically about at the gurneys of sheet-covered corpses that surrounded him in the room—clearly he was disturbed by them—then escaped back to his book.

The corpsmen outside the window snorted and choked back laughter.

"What's going on?" I asked.

"Shhhh. Just watch."

After a few minutes I was surprised to hear a low painful moan from one of the sheeted gurneys. Then I understood.

The young corpsman dropped his book on the desk. His eyes rolled. He turned down the radio and listened intently.

Nothing.

After a few minutes, he turned up the radio again and picked up his book, but his eyes kept roving above the pages.

Presently, the sound came again. A bit louder this time, more painful.

The corpsman sat up and turned off the radio. Eyes wide, he rose and edged his way through the gurneys containing the fruits of war, studying each body bag and sheet. He walked all around the room, stopping to listen, eyes darting. Finally, he shook his head hard to clear it. Squaring his shoulders, he returned to his desk. The graveyard shift in a morgue was no time for fancy creative imagination.

He left the radio off this time when he picked up his book.

*"Ohhhhhh . . ."*

It was not his imagination. He grabbed the field phone and almost cranked the handle off it.

"Get a doctor over here right now," he shouted. "One of these dudes is still alive."

He hung up and backed against the wall to wait, like a grunt about to fire his final protective line. One of the corpsmen outside the window waited a few minutes, then composed himself and walked around to the door.

"What's wrong?" he asked, rubbing his eyes sleepily.

The new morgue corpsman was so glad to have company he looked about ready to pounce on the visitor and hug him.

"One of these folks is still alive," he explained, pointing toward the back of the room. Dim bulbs cast thin-legged shadows from the gurneys.

"What are you talking about? They've all been checked by doctors before they were sent here."

"I *heard* him moan."

"Oh, *that,*" said our corpsman. "That's just air escaping the lungs. They all do that when rigor mortis sets in."

The new guy looked relieved. "I remember hearing about it," he said. "I just didn't expect it, is all."

"Think you can handle it now?"

"Yeah. Sure. I'm okay."

The pencil mark did not look okay. He looked like an

exclamation point. He scooted his desk near the door and perched on the edge of his chair, watching and listening. After a while, he picked up his book and started to read.

*"Ohhhhhhh, God!"*

The book flew across the room, pages fluttering like a bird crippled in flight. The corpsman grabbed the field phone and cranked it frantically.

"I'm *telling* you. One of these guys is still *alive*. I heard him *talk*."

The phone operator was in on the prank. After a short time, our corpsman again went around the corner and entered the morgue, looking irritable.

"Now what's the problem?"

"I heard him say, 'Oh, God.' "

"You just think you heard it. The muscles contract in the chest cavity and they make strange noises when the air expels."

"Oh. Well . . . look, man, can't you just stay here with me for a few minutes and listen for yourself?"

"I've got another early shift tomorrow. I've got to get some sleep. Don't worry about it. Just ignore it."

The pencil mark remained in exclamation against the wall. After a while, he found the courage to gather himself into a question mark and sit down at his desk.

*"Ohhhhhh."*

The thin corpsman turned on the radio. He turned it up loud. His glasses made his eyes wide and staring, like an owl's.

Then it happened. The sheets on one of the gurneys deepest in the shadows at the back of the Quonset fluttered. The corpsman sprang to his feet.

The corpse sat upright on its gurney.

The corpsman's nerves were so jangled that he hardly made sense on the telephone.

Our corpsman put on a long-suffering air. "What's wrong *this* time?" he demanded.

The new guy pointed a trembling finger. "Look at that motherfucker there. The dude sat *up*."

Our corpsman gave it a casual glance.

"It happens all the time," he said. "Is this the first night you worked here?"

The pencil mark nodded so vigorously his glasses bounced on his nose.

"That explains why you're so nervous. Look, I told you it was just muscle contractions."

He strode to the "corpse" still sitting upright underneath the sheets and forced it flat again by holding its legs and pushing down on the chest.

"You have to shove 'em back down when it happens," he instructed. "Otherwise, we can't fit 'em in the shipping boxes in the morning and the chief gets pissed. Understand?"

The boot looked embarrassed. "I guess so," he said, still uncertain.

"I told you I have to get some sleep. Do you think you can handle it yourself now?"

"I–I guess so."

Our corpsman was snickering behind his hand when he rejoined us to watch through the window. The new man was too unsettled to do anything except perch on the edge of his chair. Breezes sniffing around the eaves of the Quonset caused him to sit even straighter and listen. The settling and creaking of the building made him start. He was like a coiled spring waiting for something to strike his release.

He leaped to his feet the instant the "corpse" sat back up with a loud moan. The sheet fluttered. In the shadows it appeared indistinct and surreal, like a ghost.

At first, the corpsman met the emergency by bouncing around like a ping pong ball. He reached for the telephone, thought better of it, jerked his hand back, and darted for the door.

He halted in mid-stride, remembering. He slowly turned. Closing his eyes, he took a deep breath and opened one eye. The ghost remained. He opened the other eye and took another deep breath, bracing himself. Summoning all his courage, he squared his shoulders and advanced on the corpse that refused to rest like the others.

As he had been instructed, he reached out, but hesitantly, to force the "dead man" flat on its gurney. Had he been cognizant of anything other than the bizarre problem confronting him, he would doubtlessly have heard the snufflings and sniggerings from outside the window.

He forced the stiff to lie flat. He turned to leave.

The "dead man" sprang upright.

The corpsman hesitated, eyes wide behind the thick glasses, and slowly turned.

He reached for the dead man.

The dead man reached back and snatched his wrist in a vice grip.

The howl of terror that rattled the roof of the hut could have been heard on the other side of Marble Mountain as the new corpsman turned into an arrow and shot out the door and disappeared into the Vietnam night with a pounding of feet and a hearty, *"Jesus God!"*

# Chapter 28

I CHECKED OUT of the hospital. The duty corpsman strained to read the name tag on my faded utilities. I handed him my discharge card.

"Roberts," I said.

He consulted his clipboard. "It says here you're to report to your regiment headquarters at Da Nang."

"What for? My platoon's across the road at MAG-16."

He shrugged. "I just work here."

I hitched a ride to the airbase on a six-by that dropped me off in front of a sandbagged tent.

"You're a sniper, right?" asked the sergeant behind the desk.

That was news to me. "I am?"

"That's what it says here," he said, stabbing a finger at a clipboard. Everything official in the Marines was recorded somewhere on a clipboard. "You were designated a sniper by your company as of August last year."

Then I understood. "That was because I'm an AR man with bipods for the infrared scope."

"Roberts, we got a list here of designated snipers in the regiment. Your name is on it. You're a sniper."

So I was a sniper. What did I have to worry about? This was only Vietnam . . .

The sniper rifles were big-game rifles off the rack—30.06 Model 70 Winchesters, bolt action, with Unertl scopes. A number of Marines from regiment, selected apparently the same way I was, went to school to learn how to use the rifles and to hunt the most dangerous game of all—man. My partner was a little Chicano from East L.A. named Sal Rodriguez.

The Winchesters were good with long fields of fire. Otherwise, at shorter ranges, a standard M-14 worked just as well. The M-14 worked even better, in fact, with running targets since the target kept running out of the Winchester scope and you couldn't follow it. Half of the rice field shots we subsequently made in the Da Nang enclave could have been made better with the open sights on an M-14.

Sal and I drew an area of operations with the First Marine Division across the Yen River near Hill 22. Our job was to go out on night patrols and stay behind to zap any dinks we caught sneaking back to their holes at dawn. We were to operate the same way against the gooks as gook snipers had been operating against us. It seemed like a good thing, a fitting way to draw an eye for an eye.

One night we dropped behind to set up on a large mound of dirt that looked like a small Rock of Gibraltar. It was about twenty-five meters high with steep sides and just enough room at the top for two men to hide prone in a tuft of grass. Sal and I scrambled to the top while our security rifleman set up at the base in elephant grass to protect our rear. I clamped a pair of M-14 bipods to the barrel, extended the legs, chopped some grass to hide the weapon's silhouette, then rolled over on my back and lay staring at the stars with Sal, each of us caught up in our own thoughts as we waited for dawn and the VC to start moving back to their rat traps and tunnels to hide for the day.

I thought about Rita and felt a tinge of jealousy hard to control at the thought of some Stateside Jodie watching the stars with her while I was here. I forced myself to stop thinking.

The sun came up. There were shadows. Then the rice fields grew out of the shadows like green squares gridded by dikes. The rains were more infrequent nearing the end of the monsoon season, and it was already hot. It hadn't cooled off much during the night, and there was no breeze. Sal scanned the fields, then put down the binoculars and swiped sweat out of his eyes with his sleeve. Suddenly, he stared, snatched the glasses again, and locked onto something. He sank closer to the ground.

"Check this shit out," he murmured, exhaling slowly. I gently pushed the grass away from the rifle to get to the scope.

"Eleven o'clock—seven hundred meters," Sal said.

I pulled the butt stock against my shoulder and picked my spot on the cheek piece to get the best picture from the scope. A dike and a line of jungle jumped at me. I scanned, slowly, until I picked up the first gook. I went down the line, counting them. Seven gooks walking along a dike toward the Tuy Loan River like they were out for their morning constitutional. We had strict orders still not to fire at anything unless we saw weapons. There were no "free fire zones" as there were later in the war. No problem with shooting these, though.

"Okay. I see weapons. I'm going for Tailend Charlie."

I had read this book once about an American sniper in WWII who always picked off the last man in a column so he wouldn't spook the others until he could get off another shot or two.

I laid crosshairs at the top of the last man's head, anticipating bullet drop at this range. The man was young and bare-headed with an SKS thrown over one shoulder. His skin glowed almost red in the morning sunlight, like an Indian's. He also looked tired.

He turned his head and stared almost directly into my

eyes; I knew he could not possibly see me. It was a little strange nonetheless, looking eye to eye like that through the scope.

*So long, shithead.*

I took up trigger slack—and fired.

An invisible fist slammed out of the sky and knocked him off the dike into the rice paddy where he splashed around like a wounded duck, alerting the others who had not heard the shot. Two of the gooks jumped into the rice to grab their comrade while the others raced along the dike toward a tree line by the river.

"Watch your breathing," Sal advised. "Your muzzle is rising and falling."

I clenched my breath inside my teeth and tasted salt from sweat. Sweat blurred my vision through the scope. I blinked and the two gooks dragging the other came clear, like a TV picture suddenly in focus. I fired. A little geyser of water erupted in front of them. Sal was watching through the glasses.

"Too much lead," he exclaimed. "Roberts, nail the fuck-heads! They're getting away."

The VC were leaving a wake of water behind them as they dragged their fallen friend through the rice. Each VC had him clasped by an arm. The wounded man's head lolled forward and down into the water. If my bullet hadn't killed him, I thought, then they would surely finish him off by drowning.

"Give 'em hell," Sal cried in exasperation.

I squeezed off again and saw one of the dinks stumble and grab himself—but they kept going. Why was it you could shoot these little bastards with an elephant gun and they'd still get up and run off while an American would die from a little piece of shrapnel you could hardly see?

"They're getting away," Sal screamed in the excitement. "Fuck it. I'm gonna open up, too. At least we can scare the shit out of 'em."

The private at the base of the Rock of Gibraltar scrambled up to join us and get in his licks. Sal rose to one knee to sight in with his M-14. The three of us firing made geysers in the water all around the fleeing VC. Each time I fired, the recoil jarred me off-target and I wasted time getting back on. The rifle needed to be heavier with a heavier barrel.

The VC made it into the bamboo thicket by the river and faded from sight. It was abruptly peaceful again in the morning sunlight with the rice gridded off in green squares and some birds calling from the trees behind us.

One thing you didn't do when there was just three of you was wait around for a body count. It might be *your* body *they* were counting. We slid from our perch and selected the escape route we had already picked out, cautious now lest the tables turned and *we* became the target.

It was that kind of war.

Night after night Sal and I hunted. We hunted—and we waited on a stand. Ninety percent of war, it seemed, was nothing but waiting for something to happen. I hated the waiting. Time dragged, and the dragging gave you too much time to think.

Nothing happened most of the time. We dropped off from a patrol, just Sal and I and the rifle and a rifleman for rear security, and set up somewhere and waited for dawn and the VC. We watched farmers pass in the distance with their water buffalo, or old women with baskets on their heads chewing betel nut, walking stoically in the fresh sunlight and through time that was without time for them.

It was a bonus and a few minutes' excitement, exactly as on a big game hunt, whenever we spotted VC sneaking back from their night's mischief. We turned the tables on them; now, *we* were the enemy who hid in the jungle like ghosts, who killed unseen and then vanished into the shadows of bamboo.

Killing like this was personal, not like in a firefight when it was difficult to tell who killed who. Through the scope you could see the expressions on their faces in that instant before you sent a bullet screaming into their flesh. Mostly they were young faces, some no older than sixteen. I was just nineteen, so their youth had little impact. I killed a few, Sal killed a few, and if there was any feeling to it, it was satisfaction. We were doing something personal to avenge Marines who had been killed and maimed by mines, booby traps, and snipers.

Going to the enemy on his own turf and killing him was better than waiting until he came on yours. We were seeing the enemy—and he was ours.

There was a moon round and full on the horizon—a sniper's moon—when the little team set up one night not far away from a small Buddhist temple with ornate carvings on the roof that reminded me of Mieu Dong and the ARVN Rangers. The temple had been built in isolation along a path well used by villagers during the day.

We had barely settled down for another wait before rear security came belly crawling through the grass, signaling by drawing the edge of his palm across his throat. He had not been asleep. I passed the signal along to Sal. Danger.

Two forms walked by on the trail directly in front of us and paused near the temple. They looked around in the moonlight, like bootleggers, before one squatted quickly and, to our surprise, lifted the camouflaged mat lid to a spider trap or tunnel. Both men disappeared into the hole and the lid fell back into place behind them. If we had not been watching, we would never have seen it.

"Now what?" our security wondered.

Tunnels had been known to contain vast stores of arms and provisions and were sometimes large enough to hold a battalion headquarters or an entire underground hospital. I had heard stories about one tunnel with more than ten miles of passageways and rooms, all of them underground. It could have hid—and possibly did—an NVA regiment.

Obviously, we couldn't chance carrying out any sniping from here.

"We may as well move," I decided. "The night's a waste now."

Sal shook his head. "It ain't if we can take out them two."

I thought about it. "Maybe it's just a little hole. We could try fragging 'em before we got the hell out."

"Let's do it."

Huddling like conspirators, we formulated a plan, whispering directly into each other's ears. The best plans are always simple. We elected to spread out and approach the tunnel entrance from three sides. The security man wanted to do the fragging, since he had never killed a VC, so Sal and I would cover him while he slipped up and planted an egg on the trapdoor.

We rose silently out of the bushes and spread quickly to surround the target. The security man had not been in-country long, but he took a deep breath and went ahead of us. I was afraid he would fall through before he located the concealed entrance, but after a minute's search he found it and signaled.

I saw him place the grenade on the mat and run. I slid down an embankment on my belly to escape shrapnel and hide my face from the blast of light. The concussion shook the ground.

As soon as the grenade exploded, Sal ran back up and slammed another grenade into the smoking hole with all his strength so it would bounce around and could not be picked up and tossed back out. The *whump!* of that explosion came from deep underground. Sal flopped on his belly and took a quick peek inside before he came running.

"It's a goddamned tunnel," he shouted. There was no longer any call for whispering. "I don't know if we got anybody or not. Let's *di di* the fuck outa here, amigos."

We took off across the paddies to the nearest island of jungle. In this strange war, we were either chasing or being chased, sniping or being sniped, fragging or being fragged. It was like a *Mad Magazine* comic strip called "Spy Vs. Spy" in which the guys in white and the guys in black were always doing atrocious things to each other but neither ever winning. I sometimes wondered who kept score on the war to tell who *was* winning—and *how* it was they kept score.

We slept during the days and with the fall of night we packed up our rifle and scope, like shift workers packing a lunch, and went back to work. It was a job. Like Sal quipped, it kept us busy and off the street corners. He grew up in the barrios of Los Angeles and knew about street corners.

"I've shot at more splibs in L.A. than I have dinks over here," he said once after a disappointing night's work.

We were just becoming skillful at the job when the asshole in the map room started moving pins again and all the regimental snipers were called back to Da Nang for evaluation. The snipers gathered outside a tent to compare kills and methods before an officer approached carrying the inevitable clipboard.

"Everybody made it back," he announced, "except for a couple who ran into trip wires. You guys did a damned good job. The program looks like a success and we may be expanding it. In the meantime, some of you will stay here while those of you on loan will return to your units. Congratulations. You proved we can fight the VC on his own terms—and fight just as well as he does."

Since I was on loan, that meant I would be returning to my outfit. I had not had any word about Frenchy and Yates and O'Brien in weeks. A couple of the snipers had been assigned to work with the Ninth Marines.

"Them fuckers are *crazy*," said the sniper named Franks. "That's their reputation. They go out on patrols with just seven or eight guys. That's 'cause that's all they got left. When they say send out a squad, that *is* a squad."

He shook his head in amazement.

"Know what they're calling 'em?" he asked. "They're calling 'em 'The Walking Dead.' "

# Chapter 29

THE CONVOY RODE A FOG of bitter dust to a halt where Third Battalion was preparing to move out of Marble Mountain on another sweep. Shoulder slinging my M-14, returning to the outfit, I swung down from one of the six-bys cargoing arms and supplies and onto the road, next to which a long column of Amtracks was revving up and loading up with dusty-faced gyrenes. It was typical confusion—sergeants and officers running about swinging their arms and trying to shout above the roar of the track engines, squads making last-minute checks of weapons and equipment, tracks and trucks and ONTOS getting in each other's way and bouncing around, kicking up dust and smoke and making a racket that must be keeping Ho Chi Minh himself awake and alerting every VC in the TAOR that something was coming down.

There was a hand-lettered sign on a tall post by the side of the road. It seemed the Ninth had not only been stuck with its new name, it had appropriated it with a sort of perverse pride. I read the sign through the dust:

This area secured by the 9th Marines,
Compliments of The Walking Dead.

Crowning the post was a yellowing human skull that grinned down upon all the activity as though it knew secrets.

I slogged forward along the column, coughing from the dust, until I located Mike Company with Second Platoon on point. Phil Leslie was busy building a wall of sandbags around the top of an Amtrack. O'Brien tossed him up a full bag, then stretched his back and looked around. A grin spread like a flash across the swarthy face. Leslie looked up and also grinned.

"Sonofabitch."

I was home. "You guys miss me?"

"Jee-suz Kee-rist, Roberts. You been gone somewhere, have you?"

"When the local VC find out I'm back, they'll all run away and you guys will be safe."

Leslie had his shirt off. His body and face were caked with dust. He dropped off the Amtrack to shake hands. "Our map pin just changed to red," he joked.

Corporal Bellot, a man of few words, came up and greeted me with a slap on the back and then got down to business.

"That's our track Leslie and O'Brien are prettying up. Stow your gear inside and give us a hand. We're pulling out mosh skoshe and heading upriver around the Horseshoe. I guess when the skipper feels like it we'll turn up one of the banks in an assault line."

"That's it?"

"What else do mushrooms need to know?"

I looked around. Black Bruce and Smitty the farm boy and O'Brien the Arab and Frenchy and the core of the old bunch was still intact. Bellot read my mind, however. He glanced away a moment. Word had already gotten around that he had been offered a field commission, but had turned it down. I thought I knew the reason. While Sergeant Shireman felt personally responsible for the platoon, Bellot felt that same responsibility for those of us remaining in the squad.

"As you can see," Bellot said gloomily, "there's a lot fewer of us now."

"I already heard about The Walking Dead. What happened?"

The skin stretched over his face so you could see the skull almost as clearly as the skull on the post down the road.

"Same old shit," he said. "Booby traps, snipers, mortar rounds, sick, and so on. We still aren't getting any replacements. It looks like they sent us Raglund to win the war on."

He shrugged.

"It's just as well," he continued. "That way we don't have a bunch of new boot recruits to worry about."

Melancholy was something Bellot rarely entertained. I was starting to feel bad.

*"Saddle up, you assholes! Mount them fucking beasts."*

Sergeant Shireman. He came tramping down the line, his helmet buckled square and solid on his head and his M-14 tight and ready. He was grinning, the sonofabitch.

"Roberts, cut that shit-eating grin and mount up. R & R's over for you, shit-for-brains."

But he kept grinning and I kept on, too. Black exhaust belched from the Amtracks, gates clanged shut, horns blew. I crowded into our Amtrack with the squad, like a litter of puppies in a bitch's steel belly. It had been a long time since I had felt like grinning so much. Frenchy gripped my arm. O'Brien winked.

We all knew it. As long as Sergeant Shireman survived, we, the core of Second Platoon, The Walking Dead, would keep on walking.

I wondered if Sergeant Shireman's first name really was *Sergeant*.

# Chapter 30

APRIL CAME and the monsoons were ending except for the evening rains and an odd tropical shower. The wind was dryer and cooler, but the hard sheen to the noonday sky promised the blistering summer sun could not be far away. Rumors circulating among the mushrooms—Sergeant Shireman confirmed they were fairly reliable, as far as rumors went—held that the battalion would be rotated home intact before July. None of us dared repeat the rumors except in trusted company, and then only in whispers, for fear they would be taken away from us. The Crotch gives—and the Crotch takes away.

Still, there was hope.

Mike Company got a new commander before the battalion moved from Marble Mountain. He was the rear-echelon type who always looked more appropriate in the officers' club boasting of his exploits than actually in the field doing them. His uniform was new and crisp and tailored tight-legged to fit into polished jungle boots, and he had that officer's hump on the shoulders at the base of his neck from going around with his chin thrust out. The thing that astounded everyone was that he was so proud of being a captain that he wanted everybody to know about it, including, it seemed, the enemy. He wore his captain's railroad tracks on his helmet and on his collar. Almost no one else in Vietnam wore rank in the field. Too tempting a target for the VC.

Spit-and-polish Captain Bob Stone almost drowned an Amtrack filled with Second Platoon Marines on his first company-sized operation.

The green metal boxes with their fighting cargo churned upstream against a muddy river current flowing beneath a hot clear sky. Second Platoon's three squads—or at least what remained of three squads—had crowded into the second amphibian, Bellot's squad riding outside on top behind sandbags to act as security while the other two squads suffered inside the monster's hot belly below waterline. I rode next to the driver's cupola, my automatic rifle pointing toward the river bank. Ready to waltz Matilda if I had to.

Captain Stone ordered the tracks to leave the river up a steep clay bank. Although the platoon leaders protested, the new CO insisted.

"Dumb sonofabitch," Lieutenant Rowe muttered.

The lead track had no problem climbing the clay bank, but it watered down the clay as it went, making it as slippery as grease on glass. Second Platoon's track swung wide and the driver goosed his engine to pick up speed. It lumbered forward, hit the bank, its tracks clawing, and started up, spinning mud.

Halfway up, the machine began losing ground. Engine roaring, the beast slipped back toward the water. It became lodged with the back half in the river and the forward half on land at such an angle that darkwater gushed through the two rear escape hatches, flooding the troop compartment and forcing the vehicle even more snugly against the clay bank.

It could not obtain sufficient traction to go either forward up the bank or backward into the river.

It was sinking fast.

The men inside set up a howl as soon as they recognized their predicament. On top, some of Second Squad began abandoning ship, jumping to safety on the river bank and scrambling away to give those below deck access to the one-man escape hatches, while others threw sandbags and other equipment into the river to lighten the load and to clear the top cargo doors. The machine was sitting at too high an angle for the bow gate to open.

There was no way two squads could escape through the hatches one man at a time.

The river's hungry current tugged at the monster. The exhaust pipes disappeared below water, gurgling. If the engine flooded, the bilge pumps quit—and the Amtrack *would* sink.

Men continued to abandon ship, helping each other. But not fast enough. The water rose inside, pouring in through every opening.

It was only at the last moment, with the Marines inside still trapped in the flood and struggling to get out, that another Amtrack chugged up. Its crew quickly passed a cable to the beached one. It was tied off between the two machines. Engines shrieked in a final effort.

The grounded Amtrack lurched, shuddered. It appeared it would sink before it slipped free. Marines were still scrambling through the escape hatch one at a time when the machine broke loose and floated, bobbing into the current with a miraculous three inches of freeboard left.

The trapped squads cheered.

"We're getting too short for this shit." Dave Bruce sighed.

When the Amtracks finally landed on a nearby sandy beach to disgorge the rest of the platoons, Captain Stone was already ashore standing in the open next to his radioman trying to read a large unfolded map. He looked confused. The company gunnery sergeant patiently went up to him, took the map and folded it and pointed to the north.

Looking disgusted, Sergeant Shireman nudged Bellot. "Just as soon as we can explain to this boot skipper where the hell we are on the map and which fucking way is north," he said, "then we'll be moving out. If some gook don't get him first."

Captain Stone's popularity went down from there.

Third Battalion got its pin moved and humped south and dug in at a village marked on the map as An Hoa. Engineers and Seabees bulldozed sand walls and fighting parapets for a new battalion base camp, behind which we erected hard-backed tents. Tanks and ONTOS were set up to support strategic areas of the perimeter.

From this battalion base camp, line companies went out to construct their own base camps. Platoons then ran their patrols out from the company base camps and set up temporary PPBs, or Platoon Patrol Bases, from which squads operated recon and combat patrols. The platoons returned to company base every two or three days for rest and refitting. The system was like a multileafed clover extending ever outward with battalion headquarters in the center.

The terrain was unusually dry and sandy with little pine trees dotting the landscape, a welcome change from flooded rice paddies and jungle clumps. That it was easy to hide punji pits in sand was the only bad thing.

Before we left battalion, Sergeant Shireman assembled the platoon.

"Gather 'round, shitheads. This is what I want: Each man will draw all the ammo and grenades he can carry, including each a two-hundred round belt of M-60 machine gun ammo. Store it in seabags in your tents."

He smirked. He trusted no one outside the platoon.

"That's just in case the slant-eyed cuntlickers cut us off here and we can't be resupplied from Da Nang. We can kick ass 'til the cows come home."

We didn't talk much anymore about kicking ass. We were getting to be short-timers. All we wanted to do was survive for a couple of more months until the battalion got rotated home. Kicking ass was for the newbys—and for Sergeant Shireman. Sergeant Shireman would probably stay as long as there was a war, which, if things kept going like they were, would be for a very long time.

No sooner had Mike Company moved out to its base camp and built bunkers and laid concertina wire than Bellot returned from a meeting looking stunned. He swept off his helmet and scratched his head.

"You heard me," he said. "Captain Stone wants a personnel inspection in company formation in twenty minutes."

Protests ran through the squad. "No-fuckin'-body holds personnel inspection in the field in Vietnam."

"Captain Stone does. He says our uniforms look like shit and our boots ain't been shined."

"*What!*"

"Just get ready." Bellot sighed. "We all asked the gunny what the fuck was going on, but the gunny said it was because he was a dumbfuck boot captain straight from the guard detachment at Treasure Island."

That brought out a collective moan. The guard detachment was spit-and-polish garrison troopers carried to the last degree.

It had been so long since Mike Company stood formation that it became more cluster fuck than formation. It didn't matter. Sergeant Shireman had a little surprise waiting for the new CO.

Captain Stone showed up in creased utilities and spit-shined boots. He collected the company gunnery sergeant and proceeded down the ranks of First Platoon. The captain was not a happy man about what he saw. He grew red in the face and the hump at the base of his neck bunched up like a bull's.

"When was the last time you cleaned this weapon, Marine?" he demanded.

"This morning, sir."

"This weapon is *filthy*."

He moved on in precise square movements.

"When was the last time those boots saw polish?" he asked another grunt.

"December, sir, I think."

211

The captain blinked like he had been hit between the eyes. "December . . . you *think?*"

"Yes, sir. It was December. I'm sure it was."

The captain passed on, precisely, gigging men for haircuts and dirty weapons and torn pockets and unshined boots, as though the unit had never left Pendleton.

"This is not a fighting unit," he scolded the platoon leader when he finished, speaking loudly so everyone could hear the depths of his displeasure. "Lieutenant, you *will* turn this ragtag outfit into a fighting unit. Do I make myself clear?"

"Yes, sir."

"A clean, squared-away, sharp-looking, *Marine* fighting unit."

"Yes, sir."

Second Platoon was next. Lieutenant Rowe met the captain to escort him. Sergeant Shireman stood in front of the formation.

Captain Stone stopped and stared. His chin stuck out and his neck veins bulged. There were big gaps in the platoon ranks where men were missing. The captain almost marched directly through Sergeant Shireman. The sergeant held his ground, his eyes locked straight ahead.

"Why aren't your people dressed and covered?" Captain Stone angrily demanded.

Sergeant Shireman did not blink. "They are, sir."

"Then what are those gaps for, Sergeant?"

"They're for the people who aren't here, sir."

The captain swallowed. Red crept dark up his neck. "I said I wanted *everybody* in this formation," he shouted, spewing into Sergeant Shireman's face. "Just where are these people?"

Sergeant Shireman still did not blink. His hawk's eyes remained unchanged, fixed straight ahead. After a short silence, his voice carried and hung over the entire company, then bounced around through Second Platoon, picking out all the empty spaces like one of those little sing-along-with-Mitch balls that were sometimes used in musicals.

"Dead, sir," Sergeant Shireman said.

An even longer silence followed. The captain stared at Sergeant Shireman. He stared at his feet. He stared away. His face muscles began working with a question that he did not want to ask in front of the men but which became suddenly so important that he had to ask it. If there were gaps like that in the enlisted ranks, then surely there were similar gaps among the officers.

Captain Stone turned from Sergeant Shireman to the gunny, who stood with Lieutenant Rowe, attempting to control his expression. He tried to keep his voice low.

"Gunny, how many company commanders have you had?"

The gunny spoke up deliberately for everyone to hear. "How many COs, sir? You're number four, sir. They generally last about three months."

That was Mike Company's last personnel inspection.

After the near-drowning of Second Platoon in the river and the personnel inspection, Captain Stone spent a lot of time in his bunker, having picked up scuttlebutt that his own company had placed a price on his head and was in competition to see who could frag him. When he left the bunker at all, he left it in the company of either the gunny or one of the platoon leaders. A squad leader from Third Platoon happened to overhear a conversation between Captain Stone and the gunny which soon picked up embellishment as it passed around.

"They're out to get me," Captain Stone said.

"Who, sir?"

"The men. I won't come back from the next mission."

"Nonsense, sir. The men just don't understand you is all."

"I understand *them*. I want them court-martialed."

"Who, sir?"

"Whoever is going to kill me."

"No one's going to frag you, sir."

"They're out to get me," Captain Stone insisted.

Like everyone else, creased tight-legged utilities or not, Captain Stone caught the trots. Unfortunately for him, the four-holer shitter was located about fifty meters out in front of the wire. The urgency of his condition demanded he leave the safety of his bunker frequently, and alone, since he dared not ask the gunny or his officers to accompany him *there*.

The grunts chuckled every time the skipper erupted from his command center to rush straddle-legged and in obvious pain through the wire, unbuttoning his trousers before he reached his destination in order to be ready.

Adding to Captain Stone's consternation and discomfort, a sniper in the tree line started zinging rounds next to the latrine, high enough not to hit the suffering occupant but close enough to send the distraught officer hurtling out, dragging up his pants and bearing only slight resemblance to the squared-away boot captain who had held inspection just a short time ago.

Sergeant Shireman stood in the door of his tent and silently lighted a cigarette before he grinned with secret good humor and went back inside.

Although Mike Company had two men in an observation post placed in the same tree line with the sniper, the Marines kept saying they could not locate him.

# Chapter 31

CLOUDS HAD BEEN CHASING each other across the sky like frolicking white sheep all morning. In the afternoon the black sheep came out and they bunched up and blotted out the sun. A darkness settled over the land, the way I had once read about in the Bible, and with the darkness a gloominess that awoke the furry little creature alive in my gut. It kneaded its claws just enough to cause a vague uneasiness, an awareness that the balance of things was not quite right.

The rain began just as the platoon entered the green bamboo on the edge of the village. Huge drops splattered on the dusty bamboo leaves, making clean round spots and rattling like something huge but invisible had passed through. Immediately the downpour followed, drumming on my helmet and almost obscuring from view O'Brien and Frenchy to my right and Yates and Smitty to my left. Once again the war had a way of narrowing down to become focused on who was immediately to your left or right and nothing else.

Wet clay earth sucked at my boots, reluctant to let go each step. The platoon entered the village on line, sweeping, weary. Bedraggled chickens scurried away with their heads tucked against the rain and their bare asses up. Children and old women watched us from their doorways.

With Smitty, I checked two or three hootches, kicking over urns and upsetting rice baskets to check for enemy weapons or documents, while the occupants regarded us with narrowed unwavering eyes. We checked a gate for trip wires and booby traps, then slogged across a small opening, like a village green, our helmets bowed to shield the hard rain from our faces. An overhang on a small concrete temple provided a moment's respite from the weather. The rain lent the hamlet that mystical, otherworldly quality always associated with the Orient.

Smitty lighted a cigarette, cupping his hands, and took three or four quick pulls before pinching off the coal and stuffing the butt into his pocket to save. Tommy Shands with his grenade launcher and another grunt floated by. They glanced at us and kept going.

The downpour slackened to a light sprinkle. Smitty and I stepped out from shelter and continued through the village.

Gunfire cracked from ahead—three quick shots from an M-14. You could tell the difference in the sounds of the M-14 and an AK. Smitty's safety clicked off as we hurried forward, rounding a hut in time to see O'Brien slowly approaching a VC who was down on his knees in the mud with his hands outstretched toward the Arab.

O'Brien's bullets had shattered the VC's left knee as he ran from the hut. Blood mixed with water was quickly forming a puddle. Frenchy stood back a ways with his rifle pointed. O'Brien had his weapon thrust out toward the wounded enemy.

"*Chieu hoi . . . Chieu hoi . . . ?*" the VC pleaded, face upthrust.

The Viet Cong looked young, certainly no older than twenty. He wore shortened black pajama bottoms with no

216

shirt. His ribs showed. An AK-47 lay in the mud just out of his reach.

"*Chieu hoi . . . Chieu hoi . . . ?*"

"*Chieu hoi,* my ass," O'Brien growled, aiming his weapon at the gook's good knee. "Fuck you. We ain't the god-damned Army."

All mercy had left O'Brien's swarthy face. Frenchy saw it too, recognized something there.

"O'B-san?" Frenchy said. "We can get zee doc over here. He can patch him up and send him to zee rear for interrogation."

O'Brien's rifle did not waver. Terror filled the young VC's face. Both arms reached and he began pleading tearfully in rapid Vietnamese, begging for his life.

"O'Brien?" said Frenchy. "O'Brien, this is not zee way."

"Fuck him," said O'Brien. "Get his weapon."

Frenchy retrieved the AK, then stepped back. His eyes never left O'Brien. O'Brien's never left the gook.

There was something dark in O'Brien's eyes, sinister and smoldering. The VC saw it, too, and recognized it, for he stopped pleading and simply settled back on his haunches. The pressure sent blood squirting from his knee. Terror on the soldier's face turned to acceptance of whatever fate came. Rain swept into his upturned face, but he did not blink.

O'Brien shot the gook's other leg out from under him, turning the knee into hamburger and dropping the VC face down. The dink screamed in pain, a long, blubbering scream that ended with his teeth smashed into the mud. The scream became a mewling.

The muzzle of O'Brien's M-14 slowly centered on the gook's head. The unforgiving look on the Marine's face had not softened.

"O'Brien, no."

"Shut the fuck up, Frenchy. This shitbag is mine."

The Vietnamese lifted his face from the mud. He gazed past his pain deep into O'Brien's eyes with an understanding that surprised and shocked. O'Brien gazed back, unflinching. While they measured each other, the hard rain started again, drumming through the bamboo and diluting the VC's blood as fast as it poured from his wounds. The gloom deepened. My furry creature clawed at my insides.

Smitty seemed mesmerized by the scene. I grabbed his arm and tugged.

"Let's go, man," I urged.

The rain separated us from the rest of the world, walling us off from everything outside.

"Let's go, Smitty. O'Brien can handle this."

"Do you know what he's going to do?" Smitty demanded.

"Smitty, let's go."

O'Brien remained frozen in place, not even blinking behind his rain-swept glasses.

"No. O'Brien, no," was all Frenchy could think to say, but O'Brien was past the point of hearing. He had met the enemy face to face.

I led Smitty away quickly. Both of us froze when the single shot sounded in the rain, muted by it until a second later we could not be sure we had heard it at all. Smitty stared straight ahead.

"What was that?" he asked too quickly, not really wanting to know.

I kept walking.

"What was that?"

I paused. "Remember the two wiremen they found strung up by their heels at Duong Son with their balls jammed in their mouths?" I asked.

Smitty returned a quizzical look. "Yeah."

"So does O'Brien."

# Chapter 32

SECOND PLATOON MOVED to set up a three-day PPB south of The Horseshoe in the area of a village complex known as Phuong Ho, which Marines referred to as Booby Trap Row. We rode tanks until the scraggly pines grew thick enough to hide VC antitank gunners and the tankers turned back. We humped the rest of the way into a place so like a fort that I immediately dubbed it Fort Zinderneuf.

It was a small square surrounded by eight-foot-tall dikes and open fields of fire all around. It reminded me of a scene from *Beau Geste* in which French Foreign Legionnaires were surrounded and cut off in the middle of the Sahara.

They were all killed.

Two squads at a time would defend the fort while the third ran combat patrols to see what it could dig up. It wouldn't be hard to shake trouble out of the trees. The VC were multiplying like fleas on a village cur.

The platoon scattered around the four dike walls to dig fighting holes in the loose soil. I noticed everyone was digging deeper than before, almost as deep as at the begin-

219

ning. No one wanted to take any foolish chances of getting killed with rotation home only a few weeks away.

Frenchy was making jokes about his "portable hole," Smitty and Leslie were busy bantering about some trivial thing or another, and O'Brien was leaning on his E-tool, sweating, when a detonation at one corner of the fort sent a ball of smoke scooting toward the sky.

Gyrenes dug their faces into the earth, anticipating mortar fire. When nothing followed, we slowly rose, wondering who it was this time who struck the booby trap.

*"Corpsman! . . . Corpsman! . . . Griswold's hurt."*

Griswold was Lieutenant Rowe's radioman.

Doc Lindstrom ran by with his clothing flapping on his tall frame like Ichabod Crane's on the night of his wild ride. Marines jumped up and followed to where dust was still settling. The radioman lay sprawled on the ground at the top of the dike, blood and dust matted on his face. He moaned softly, regaining consciousness, as Doc began cutting clothing away from his wound and talking soothingly. Lieutenant Rowe radioed for a chopper Medevac.

Pete Yates poked at a crater in the ground with his rifle butt. "What the fuck is this?"

It was no ordinary explosion crater. Something had caved in. Yates poked around some more, attracting several more Marines, until he found a woven reed mat like the VC used to cover their tunnel entrances.

"Hey, Lieutenant. We got something here."

A few minutes' digging uncovered an arm sticking out of the collapsed hole. Smitty and O'Brien pulled out a scrawny body that was nothing but black rags and ground up meat mashed into a shapeless mass. They stretched it out on the ground for everyone to see. The left side of its skull was missing and the brain had been blown out, leaving a cavity.

It reminded me that the rest of the body was nothing but a life support system for the brain. When the brain was gone, there was nothing else left.

Moaning came from deeper inside the cave-in.

"There's another fucking dink in there."

220

A spider trap was a fighting position or the entrance and exit to a tunnel complex. This hole was actually a two-man cave called a "rat trap." A rat trap was where the VC went to hide for the day, coming out again at night to join their cellmates to look for the cheese.

After some more digging, we uncovered a wounded VC at the back of the rat trap. His wounds were minor, but he was almost dead from lack of oxygen. He started to revive in the fresh air.

Griswold could not talk, but we were beginning to understand what had happened. He had been chopping a tree blocking his field of fire. The tree grew next to the rat trap entrance. Apparently afraid of being discovered, the dead gook tried to toss out a grenade, but the grenade somehow hit something and bounced back inside the tunnel before it went off. The tunnel absorbed most of the blast and saved Griswold's life.

The reviving VC seemed to grow smaller and smaller as he curled around himself to escape the sweaty Marines looming tall and threatening around him. The Marines were muttering about stringing the gook up and dissecting him, maybe sticking *his* balls in his mouth. The platoon had turned into an old-fashioned lynch mob. That was the thought that entered my mind. Lieutenant Rowe tried to head it off.

"Ekstein, lay out an LZ for the chopper. We need to get Griswold outa here. The rest of you—get back to your positions."

It was too late. Ragged nerves stripped raw by a war of attrition had tuned the Marines to take out our frustrations on any victim fate made available. This VC had wounded one of us just a few weeks away from our going home. That, by God, wasn't fair.

"Sergeant Shireman?"

Sergeant Shireman leaned against the tree, watching.

No one was noticing Doc Lindstrom who, to one side of the ring of Marines around the cowering gook, was busy working on Griswold. That the first move came from him was so unexpected that not even Lieutenant Rowe acted to stop him at first. For too long now, the Doc had been patching us up. No one thought what it must have been doing to him inside until, suddenly, he bowled a pathway through the Marines to get to the gook.

He had his .45 clenched in his fist. He took a determined step, knelt, and rammed the pistol muzzle deep into the dink's mouth and cocked the hammer with a nasty *snick!* The VC sprawled on his back, limbs wide, eyes bulging. A little trickle of bloody saliva ran out the side of his mouth.

"I'll take care of the dirty little bastard. . . ." Doc muttered.

The platoon waited expectantly with bated breath. I knew the next sound would be that of Doc's trusty .45 disintegrating the gook's head into a pink mist. I felt nothing except a kind of mild curiosity that Doc, who had saved so many lives, would now be the one taking a life. We had seen so much violent death that it rated about as high on our emotional barometers as crawling out in the morning to find it raining.

The tableau of Doc Lindstrom with his Coke-bottle lenses and his sandy hair and the pistol stuck deep into the gook's throat, surrounded by a circle of unforgiving Marines, was an image that would live with me for the rest of my life.

"You number ten VC," Doc yelled, working himself up for the act.

The Vietnamese stared up the gun into Doc's Coke bottles.

"No . . . No. Numbah one Buddhist," he whimpered as best he could around the gun barrel.

"You number ten-thou dinky dow VC same-same Ho Chi Minh," Doc screamed, gagging the gook with the pistol.

"Doc, go ahead and waste the puke," someone whispered.

We *wanted* the gun to go off in revenge for all we—The Walking Dead—had suffered because of this dink and his buddies.

Doc was panting. Sweat rolled off a face transformed by

fury. It was the first time anyone had seen this side of the normally self-contained corpsman.

"Doc?"

Lieutenant Rowe's voice was low and steady, not without sympathy. He inched his way into the circle of stony-faced Marines where the life-and-death drama was playing itself out. Doc's entire body jerked when the lieutenant rested a hand gently on his shoulder.

"Easy, Doc," he said. "Your job is patching up people, not killing them."

"I'll patch his fucking ass up," Doc said, "after I waste him."

Then O'Brien the Arab was standing with the lieutenant. By now, everyone in the platoon knew about O'Brien and the gook he caught.

"Doc, it ain't worth it," O'Brien said with a sadness rising from the depths of his soul. "Doc, it ain't. I *know* it ain't."

Everyone realized the moment had passed. Some of the Marines turned and started to walk away. Sergeant Shireman was still watching bemused, as though he knew all along the gook was safe but wanted to satisfy his own curiosity about how far his men would go.

"It's okay, Doc," Lieutenant Rowe said. "Patch his ass up before the chopper gets here. Let battalion do the interrogating," he added, as though Doc was only fooling and wasn't really going to waste the gook.

Doc's eyes blinked rapidly, as though he were awaking from a trance. Then he let the hammer down on the .45 with his thumb and reholstered it. He stood up and silently trod away to get his aid bag. The gook's dark eyes followed him.

There was something depressing about a helicopter that has just left, I realized, after the Sikorsky flew in and dusted off Griswold and the wounded gook together. While it was on the ground with you, it represented a link to the twentieth century and the safety of the rear. When it left again, it made you feel more alone and isolated than ever.

Black flies swarming around the dead dink was also depressing. Some of us dug a shallow hole and buried the awful thing. We were just packing down the last E-tool of dirt on the makeshift grave when Bellot came up with a sour look. It seemed body count was not enough anymore, he said; the brass back at Da Nang wanted to see the corpse.

"*What?* You got to be shitting us," I exclaimed.

"Dig the sonofabitch up," Bellot said. "They're sending out a tank to take the gook back."

"*Why?*"

"How should I know, for Christ's sake? Whatta they tell mushrooms?"

The gook was starting to stink, lying in the hot sun, before the tank got there two hours later. A cloud of flies buzzed up from the stiff as the tank came rumbling in buttoned-up and driving like hell. It halted with a grinding sound and the hatch flew open.

"Where the hell is it?" the tank commander demanded, anxious to get back to An Hoa before the Viet Cong night set in.

"On the other side of the dike," I said.

"Bag it and strap it on the cargo rack behind the turret."

O'Brien bristled. "Fuck off. Bag the pile of shit yourself."

The tanker looked at us. "You call, we haul," he said. "That's all we do."

The platoon was in no mood for any more shit. Sergeant Shireman intervened before things got out of hand. He looked at us, then looked at the motor grate over the tank's engine, then looked back at us and winked.

"Take care of it for the rear-echelon shitbirds," he said.

Fuck a bunch of tankers. Fuck the bag. We took the body and slung it onto the motor grate. The grate was hot enough to barbecue on. The body began to sizzle.

"Better hurry up, tread-head. He won't last long," Yates yelled at the tank commander. "You might call ahead and ask the general how he likes his meat. He should be good and done by the time you get to An Hoa."

# Chapter 33

**P**ETE YATES ON POINT, the squad worked its way northeast toward a strip of grass hootches that followed a jungle line along a muddy river. Darkness would not come for an hour yet, but the sky was beginning to show night colors. We were approaching the outskirts of the village when three shots sounded, clean and sharp and cracking. Marines hit the dirt and scrambled around like tadpoles on dry ground while we tried to figure out if anyone had been hit and where the sniper was.

"There the asshole goes," somebody yelled.

A black-clad Vietnamese with a rifle jumped out of a spider hole and darted through an opening in the bamboo that surrounded the village before anyone could get a shot. It was unusual for a gook in daylight to show himself like that. But no one had been hit, so Bellot sent Hunt, Raglund, and Tommy Shands slipping through the same opening after the gook while the rest of the squad followed in short running bursts.

We were greeted by two more shots. The VC yelled

something in Vietnamese—it sounded like a taunt or a challenge—and again before any of us could react, popped out of a spider trap like a Jack-in-the-box and fled through the trees.

Frenchy chunked a grenade into the spider hole as the squad rushed past in pursuit of the VC. It went off with a muffled clap. He hesitated long enough to take a quick glance down the opening. He shrugged.

We kept going.

The furry creature inside my gut started to stir, awaking to look around. The shorter I got in Vietnam, the more apt the little creature was to take alarm at anything out of the ordinary. I was beginning to think I really might get out of Vietnam alive after all. The little creature kept alert to make sure I did.

We penetrated deeper into the village, like Custer after the Indians, I thought. Frenchy and O'Brien had their weapons clenched at the ready, their eyes darting to explore every movement. The squad seemed overcautious, as though everyone had a furry creature to contend with.

We passed some huts that looked temporarily abandoned and halted in a tree line to take a look across another clearing. There were more hootches on the other side, but these too seemed vacated. There weren't even any chickens. I smelled charcoal cooking fires, but it smelled like ashes, not smoke. Like the old movie line went: *Quiet. Yeah, too quiet.*

Bellot looked around. He didn't like it either, but he gave the signal and the squad moved forward.

There was a dry pond in the center of the clearing with the bowl cracked and chunked and only muddy in the middle. The sun turned red and hung on an invisible string an inch above the horizon, as though preparing to bolt into darkness at the first hint of danger. It drenched the clearing in red, turned the flak-jacketed and helmeted warriors red. Yates reached the pond, followed by the squad filtering after him.

All hell broke loose from the opposite tree line. The

deafening clatter of small arms fire sent bullets screaming around our ears like furious bees. The squad broke for the cover of the dry pond, sliding for home, and began returning fire.

I shot five round bursts at smoke and snapping flashes in the underbrush, quickly using up four of my seven twenty-round magazines.

"Palin—give me a bandoleer," I yelled.

"Fuck off," came the reply. Palin was always an asshole. "I'm low on ammo, too."

"Goddamnit, you're my ammo bearer, so fucking start *bearing*."

"Fuck off," he repeated. "I've got just enough left for *me*."

I let it go. I was too sick and too tired to argue. My leg might have healed, but my guts were ratty from parasites and dysentery and I still had some skin festers from minute pieces of shrapnel from the French mine that blew off Wertz's foot. I didn't have the energy left to give a fuck anymore; all I wanted was to get it over with and go home.

"Fuck you, Palin," I muttered.

The VC ceased fire as suddenly as they began. Something like a wind passed through their position, moving the bushes, as the enemy withdrew through the village.

Night was coming. Night was the enemy's friend.

Dave Bruce had received a nick across the back of his neck, red and flowing against the black of his skin. It was enough for a Purple Heart, but not serious. Doc Lindstrom wasn't on the patrol—night blindness—so Leslie put a patch on it. There were no other casualties.

Bellot stood up and studied the quickly-darkening tree line.

"It ain't right," Duminski said.

"What the fuck you mean—ain't right?" Bellot retorted with a sharpness in his voice that betrayed his own uneasiness.

Ekstein knelt beside the squad leader. "Bob, let's not go in there."

"When have we ever let a bunch of raggedy-ass gooks keep us from going where we have to go?"

"Bob, we're going home next month."

"Nobody's said that."

"We are. It ain't no sense getting somebody fucked-up now."

Physically wasn't the only way Bellot resembled a tank. He was unmovable. He looked at the tree line.

"The lieutenant wants us to patrol this village," he said. "That's what we're going to do. Let's move out."

One fire team covering the other, we rushed the rest of the way across the clearing and crept through a stand of thorny bamboo before we again met resistance.

Two closely spaced shots snapped through the trees at us. As we took cover, Leslie, who was ahead in the trees with Yates, yelled back a warning:

"Bellot—we got the fuckers in a bunker up here."

He ended with a burst of fire, and received a reply in kind from the bunker.

The red sun gave a last bloody gasp and dropped out of sight. Bellot crouched behind some bushes, his stocky figure merging in shadows, and used hand-and-arm signals to direct the squad against the bunker.

The fortification was a low dirt mound outlined to the right of one of the grass hootches. Muzzle flashes winked angrily from a shooting port. Russian AKs make a deeper, shorter bark than M-14s. Bullets plunged across an opening into our lines, biting off leaves and twigs around our heads, stealing the air from us.

The clatter and snarl of a firefight, the sheer volume of it, always amazed me. Red tracers converged on the bunker, sending up a cloud of dust where they ripped into the mound.

Bellot found Shands and pointed. Shands's first shot with his M-79 missed the firing port. The grenade sailed in a low arc and banged a brilliant flash of light on top of the bunker. He tried again. This time the missile sailed squarely through the opening. Lightning flashed inside, outlining the firing port. The bunker heaved a great sigh and settled back in a cloud of dust.

Frenchy rushed with me across the opening. We threw ourselves on the mound and crawled through the smoke and dust to the firing port, through which we thrust our rifles and sprayed the interior with automatic fire. Nothing could have survived such a raping.

But when the dust settled, all we discovered inside the bunker was a blood trail leading into an escape tunnel. Frenchy shook his head.

"Zee little bastards are hard to kill," he acknowledged.

We left the tunnel without exploring it, since none of us wanted to crawl down any dark passageways. Likely it led to an exit at the river.

"Bellot?" Ekstein asked.

Bellot was stubborn. We had a job to do, short-timers or not. He raised the lieutenant on the radio, then waved the squad forward.

"The lieutenant wants to know what those gooks are protecting," he said.

The only comment was a muttered, "Our pin has turned red."

# Chapter 34

THE VILLAGE WAS NARROW and long, scattered in clumps of huts in the bamboo along the bank of the river. The squad made its way along a narrow foot trail that edged the hamlet. Darkness settled around us, sharpening our apprehension.

My blood filled with ice crystals when the first log drum started throbbing. Not since the Valley of the Shadow of Death when the VC thought they had my patrol trapped had I heard the drums. Obviously, the VC thought they had us trapped again. The hair on my arms, at the nape of my neck, stood up as more drums joined the first, surrounding us like amplified heartbeats. The tempo increased to a frenzy, then ceased so completely that the silence crashed down like a physical thing.

Every man in the squad had frozen in his tracks.

*"Jee-suz Kee-rist!"*

After a moment's pause, the drums began again, building up to the same frenzy before letting the silence once more come crashing.

The silence did not last as long this time. It was immediately filled with whistles shrilling in the darkness of village and bamboo, and by gooks yelling orders at each other. It was obvious what had happened. Like Custer, we had been lured into a trap. At least a company of enemy soldiers—VC probably, but perhaps even NVA—had encircled us in a net from which there might be no escape.

I AIN'T GETTING OUT ALIVE!

What I regretted most was that I had been so near rotation.

Like cornered animals, we found ourselves desperately searching for a way out. Eyes fell almost simultaneously upon a small clearing to one side of the path. It was rimmed by thick bamboo and dotted with haystacks, each of which was about the height of a man and about six feet in diameter. There was nowhere else to hide, not a clump of jungle, not a streambed, not a hole, nothing within reach. Bellot made a signal and the squad ran and burrowed into the hay piles like rats.

I made sure to tuck in my feet and lay there trying to stifle a sneeze. Peeping out, I saw nothing but a silent empty hayfield in the deepening VC night and a foot trail that led into it, heard nothing except the pounding of my own heart, felt nothing except a fear made more real by the little creature clawing blood from my insides.

For the first time since arriving in Vietnam I found myself praying for darkness, for total blackness if possible, for an eclipse of moon and stars and planets. As if in answer to my prayers, it grew darker by the minute until I could barely make out the shapes of the other haystacks, each concealing a very frightened and unsettled Marine.

All around, the gooks were beating the bush for us, shouting and blowing whistles.

I caught my breath sharply and held it when a gook stalked into the hay field, passing so near O'Brien's hay that O'Brien could have reached out and tripped him. He stopped not ten meters from me and swiveled his head back and forth, looking.

Did he know where we were?

The sudden sound of his voice shouting in passable English almost caused me to bolt from the hay.

*"Marine! Hey, Marine! Tonight, Marine, you die!"*

*Up your mother's,* I thought in silent defiance. *First you die, scrotum face.* I could almost relish putting a bullet between his eyes.

I was accepting that we were going to die this close to going home. *Dying,* I thought with unsettling irony, *would have been better at the beginning.* That way we wouldn't have had to go through all this shit. Getting zapped at Cam Ne was a way of cheating the Marines out of a full tour in Vietnam.

While I watched, the gook did an insane thing. He tore the pin from a trip flare and dropped it at his feet, instantly bathing himself in a globe of bright light. At least he didn't know we were virtually at his feet.

*"Marine?"* he taunted. *"Hey, Marine? You shoot me?"*

Apparently, the fanatic was willing to sacrifice himself in order to get us. One shot would bring the hordes down on us like wild dogs on fresh meat. Shadows from the flare lurked and fluttered among the haystacks, but not a single straw moved. I heard my heart still pounding and I could almost hear O'Brien thinking, *Jee-suz Kee-rist.*

The gook loomed in the white light like a visitor from outer space until the flare hissed out with a gasping sizzle, returning the sweet night to us. Tonight, the darkness was *our* friend. I started breathing again with relief when the dink gave up and walked back toward the village.

It was only a matter of time, though, before the gooks thought of the haystacks and came back. Right now, they were too obvious. That had been our luck. I hoped it held.

The sounds of the hunt moved off to our flank into the abandoned village.

A minute later someone's hand darted into the hay and grabbed my ankle. My little furry creature almost had a heart attack.

"Hey," Ekstein whispered.

I stuck my head out to find him on his belly frantically

motioning me to silence. He pointed toward a thick bamboo fence to our rear. I could just barely make out big slugs wriggling across the ground toward it. I nodded and quickly joined them, crawling, following until I came to a small hole Ekstein had carved through the base of the fence. We slithered through it one at a time, Bellot on the other side counting to make sure everyone made it.

My breathing sounded like a wind tunnel.

There was a dry, sandy creek bed beyond the bamboo fence. I slid down the low bank head first and low-crawled on the sand, following the man in front of me. I couldn't tell who it was. The creek bed meandered in the general direction of our PPB.

I felt better and better as we left the sounds of the search behind us. I heard soft sighs of relief. Maybe our number hadn't come up after all, maybe our pin hadn't turned black.

Whatever relief we experienced was short-lived. The signal drums started pounding again. Whistles shrilled close in our rear, from the hayfield where the gooks had discovered our escape attempt.

"Bug out!" Bellot cried.

No words in the Marines for retreat? *Bug out* served just as good as any. The entire squad leaped to its feet and stampeded.

Rifle fire lent impetus to the inglorious withdrawal of valiant Second Squad. The angry little muzzle blossoms dotted the night behind us. Bullets screamed around our heads. Green tracers flashed through and kept on going ahead of us in great, long, slow curves.

Bellot carried the radio himself and was shouting into it as we ran, trying to raise some help. He couldn't get it to work.

We crossed a sandy opening studded with short pines. A frantic glance over my shoulder revealed what seemed like hordes of enemy chasing us, blossoming fire as they came.

I threw back my head and pumped my arms and—*ran!*

We temporarily lost our pursuers when we reached the rice paddies, but we dared not rest. Sweating and gasping, we slowed to a trot and jogged south toward the PPB, using the dikes for concealment. The situation wasn't the same as when we were trapped in the haystacks, but it was still desperate.

Our hopes rose, just to be dashed again when enemy artillery exploded an illumination round in the sky over our heads. We were lit up like Times Square on New Year's Eve.

"Oh, fuck, fuck, fuck!"

A crescendo of rifle fire sent us diving for cover. Miraculously, so far, none of us had been hit except for Bruce's scratch at the dry pond. Peeping over the top of the dike revealed a ragged line of enemy troops charging across the rice paddy toward us beneath the high, bright, artificial sun of the flare. They were less than three hundred meters away.

What perfect targets. We could not outdistance them in the open, I realized, thinking: *Why not take some of them with us to hell?*

"Bellot, I'm tired of this shit," I yelled.

Bellot was tired ot it, too. He gave the order to fire and maneuver. Ekstein's fire team jumped up and ran toward the platoon base while Bruce's laid down a field of fire as cover.

"Surprise, surprise, assholes!" O'Brien shrieked.

Red tracers, low, grazing, cut across the field. A couple of gooks threw up their arms and went down hard. The others scattered to wait until the illumination round dropped behind a jungle, silhouetting it in jagged terrible relief, and then plunging friend and foe alike back into darkness. I heard the VC advancing.

I was down to my last twenty-round magazine.

"I'm out," I heard Frenchy cry.

Bellot gave the word. "Move back!"

The team swept back past Ekstein's team which had set up to provide us covering fire.

"Conserve your ammo," Bellot encouraged. "This ain't a night for hand-to-hand."

We had slowed the enemy, but we hadn't stopped him. Twice more we fired and maneuvered. We were on familiar terrain, which meant the PPB couldn't be far away, although Bellot still could not make radio contact.

The question was: Could we reach the platoon before we ran out of ammo and the gooks reached us?

Hope was starting to fade when suddenly an M-60 machine gun started its deep-throated chatter. It had to be from Fort Zinderneuf. Although the squad found itself belly down in an open field caught in a crossfire between the PPB and a company of furious VC closing in for the kill, that M-60 was the most welcome sound I had ever heard.

We were going to make it. Fuck the gooks. They didn't have our number. Tommy Shands rolled joyfully onto his back and popped off his remaining grenades down range toward the enemy. The rest of us gripped frags, the only weapons remaining to us except our bayonets—and the time did not seem quite right for another bayonet charge.

Bellot finally got through to Lieutenant Rowe. *"Iron Tree Two-Niner . . . This is Six. Goddamnit, lift your fire. We're coming in."*

As soon as the stream of red tracers shifted to give us a hole, the squad sprang up and fled toward the dike fort. I was the last man to the wall. I turned and hurled my remaining grenade as far as I could throw it. As it exploded in the sand, I clambered up the dike and rolled over the edge.

*"Safe!"* Sergeant Shireman yelled in his best umpire's voice. *"What the fuck you shitbirds doing—antagonizing the local population again?"*

Blinded by sweat, my heart pumping like a one-cylinder engine from exertion and excitement and disbelief that I had made it back alive, again, I snatched off my helmet with the I KILL VC TO KEEP RITA FREE on it and used it for a chair. I sat for a long time after the VC retreated and the firefight ended, totally exhausted, my head supported in dirty hands. Around me the rest of the squad was in a similar condition.

The mushrooms were being rotated home in another month, but another month seemed a long, long time away.

*"Jee-suz Kee-rist."*

# Afterword

LANCE CORPORAL WILLIAM CRAIG ROBERTS rotated home fourteen days ahead of the rest of his battalion. Second Platoon was preparing to move out on another mission when Roberts was discovered to be extremely ill from wound complications and other medical problems stemming from parasites and dysentery. Ultimately, he received a medical disability discharge from the U.S. Marine Corps.

"How'd you like to go home?" a doctor aboard the hospital ship USS *Repose* asked me, eying my X-rays and test results.

I felt like I had been struck with a 105mm round.

"Home?"

There were times I never thought I would make it.

"You mean—Stateside? Home?"

"Your intestines have never healed properly. They never will over here. You need to be back in a milder climate immediately. When are you due to rotate?"

"My battalion is due out in two weeks."

"You'll beat it home by a week and a half. I'll set it up for you to catch a Medevac flight out of the airbase tomorrow."

The little furry creature in my gut turned over once and that was the last I heard from him.


Through a window I watched the outline of Vietnam fade below and behind as the Air Force Convair took off from the Da Nang airbase filled with sick and wounded, some of whom, swathed in bandages, lay strapped in stretchers and could not get a last look.

Scenes from the past year flashed before my eyes like a movie played in slow motion. I saw the faces of men in the platoon who were closer to me than any family could ever be because of what we had shared together—Frenchy Michaud, Roland O'Brien the Arab, Pete Yates, Smitty, Bob Bellot, Doc Lindstrom, Sergeant Shireman, George Renninger, Phil Leslie, Dave Bruce, and the others, including Nguyen Hai and his Rangers with their ducks and chickens.

I relived, for a moment, the firefights, the endless patrols, the fear of mushrooms kept in the dark and fed horse shit when some mysterious stranger moved our pin around on the map.

The pilot's cheerful voice over the intercom interrupted my reveries: "Welcome aboard the Freedom Bird. You're going home. Next stop—Clark Air Force Base, Philippine Islands."

I cheered as loudly as any of the wounded men in the belly of the Freedom Bird.


Twenty years later, Frenchy Michaud picked me up at the airport in a topless red MGA and drove through the hilly wine country of northern California. He lived in a mobile home surrounded by mountain pines and tropical plants. A GI steel helmet hanging suspended upside down from a tree branch served as a planter. On the wall of the porch facing the street was a full-size Marine Corps recruiting poster showing a tough DI in a flat-brimmed campaign hat pointing toward Frenchy's front door. The caption at the bottom directed: ENLIST HERE.

Frenchy knew where to find O'Brien at a colorful Irish bar in Berkeley frequented by bikers, students, and the wrinkled remains of old hippies.

"Jee-suz Kee-rist, Roberts."

The reunion traced back through time, the focus always on Vietnam, which had formed my generation.

"They make it look like all Vietnam vets were undisciplined shitbirds who ran around smoking dope and shooting each other," I complained over beers.

"It ees obvious," said Frenchy, "that they never knew a Sergeant Shireman."

O'Brien swiveled his head as though he were back on point, his eyes taking in the bikers, students, and hippies, few of whom had shared our experiences. Some were too young, some were protestors and draft dodgers. A mischievous gleam flashed in the Arab's eyes.

"This place," he observed loudly, "is full of commies and democrats."

I knew we were in trouble.

" 'Bout time we busted this place up, ain't it, Roberts?"